Christ's Disciple: How To Finish Strong

Christian Growth Series

Robert Lloyd Russell

Published by LCL Company NW, 2023.

Also by Robert Lloyd Russell

Bible Character Series
Samson: Spirit-Controlled to Self-Centered
Peter: Failure to Faith

Christian Concepts Series
God's Church: Christ's Pearl
God's Nature: Sonlight Sunlight
God's Child: Like a Tree

Christian Growth Series
God's Desire: How To Please God
God's Light: How To Respond
Christ's Disciple: How To Finish Strong

Christian Theology Series
Christ's Blood: 7+ Amazing Benefits
Pride: Good and Bad
Temptation: 50+ Tips

Missions
Jim Elliot: Recorded Messages

Watch for more at www.booksrlr.com.

Table of Contents

Christ's Disciple: How To Finish Strong (Christian Growth Series) ... 1

Introduction ... 3

Prolog ... 7

Chapter 1 ~ Overview ... 11

Chapter 2 ~ Foundation: Decision ... 15

Chapter 3 ~ Level 1: Decisions ... 21

Chapter 4 ~ Level 2: Thoughts ... 35

Chapter 5 ~ Level 3: Attitudes ... 51

Chapter 6 ~ Level 4: Motivations ... 59

Chapter 7 ~ Level 5: Actions ... 67

Chapter 8 ~ Level 6: Lifestyle ... 73

Chapter 9 ~ Level 7: Finish Strong ... 81

Chapter 10 ~ Nothing New ... 91

Chapter 11 ~ Heaven ... 95

Chapter 12 ~ Rewards ... 101

Epilog ... 115

Appendix A – Text Pyramid Summary ... 119

Appendix B – Scripture Pyramid Summary ... 121

Appendix C – The Simplicity of Salvation ... 123

Additional Thoughts.. 127

About the Author 129

Want Free Books?.. 131

What To Read Next 133

While every precaution has been taken in the preparation of this book, the publisher assumes no responsibility for errors or omissions, or for damages resulting from the use of the information contained herein.

CHRIST'S DISCIPLE: How To Finish Strong

First edition 7- April-2021, 1-Oct-23

Copyright © 2021 Robert Lloyd Russell

Written by Robert Lloyd Russell

Cover Photo: Public Domain: Chichén Itzá (Mayan)

Unless otherwise noted, Scripture is taken from the New King James Version © 1982. Other Scripture portions as noted are from:

King James Version (kjv) © 1909, now public domain

New American Standard Version (nasb) © 1960

New International Version (niv) © 1978

Good News Translation (gnt) © 1992

The Message (msg) © 1993

New American Standard—updated (nasu) © 1995

New Living Translation (nlt) 1996

New English Translation (net) © 1996

Notes: For consistency and clarity names and pronouns of God have been capitalized in all Bible quotations. All *emphasis* in Scripture has been added.

We hope you enjoy this book. Robert Lloyd Russell's goal is to provide high-quality, thought-provoking books that connect truth to real life needs and challenges. For more information on his other books based on Biblical interpretation and application, please visit his author's website https://booksrlr.com/

Grace and peace be multiplied to you in the knowledge of God and of Jesus our Lord, as His divine power has given to us all things that pertain to life and godliness, through the knowledge of Him who called us by glory and virtue, by which have been given to us exceedingly great and precious promises, that through these you may be partakers of the divine nature, having escaped the corruption that is in the world through lust.

2 Peter 1:2-4

If you find value in this book, please consider writing an online review. This would be very much appreciated by the author.

Introduction

Unfortunately, in today's Christian communities many are so satisfied with their ultimate destination that they neglect the importance of the journey. By so doing they are missing out on many here and now benefits of their adoption into the family of God.

I do not think it is an exaggeration to say that average Christianity today is so below par that if one truly lived the Christian life as God desires they would be considered abnormal.

Many books about living a victorious Christian life focus on the basic "spiritual disciplines" such as regular reading the Word of God, regular prayer, on-going fellowship, and so forth. While these are all critically important factors, they are not what this book is about. While the *traditional Christian disciplines are vital* there is much material readily available on that subject.

The message of this book focuses on understanding the process of forming and maintaining good habits—including, but far from limited to, the spiritual disciplines. There is a critical sequence of steps required for on-going victorious Christian living.

The title of this book, "Christ's Disciple" was chosen with care. This is not a book about being a Christian because my parents are, or because I attend church most Sundays. A disciple is an intentional follower of their leader. It is an active purposeful focus of their lives. This book is for those who with the Apostle Paul can admit:

> *'I know that all God's commands are spiritual, but I'm not. Isn't this also your experience?' Yes. I'm full of myself — after all, I've spent a long time in sin's prison. What I don't understand about myself is that I decide one way, but then I*

act another, doing things I absolutely despise. So if I can't be trusted to figure out what is best for myself and then do it, it becomes obvious that God's command is necessary.

But I need something more! For if I know the law but still can't keep it, and if the power of sin within me keeps sabotaging my best intentions, I obviously need help! I realize that I don't have what it takes. I can will it, but I can't do it. I decide to do good, but I don't really do it; I decide not to do bad, but then I do it anyway. My decisions, such as they are, don't result in actions. Something has gone wrong deep within me and gets the better of me every time.

It happens so regularly that it's predictable. The moment I decide to do good, sin is there to trip me up. I truly delight in God's commands, but it's pretty obvious that not all of me joins in that delight. Parts of me covertly rebel, and just when I least expect it, they take charge (Romans 7:14b-23 msg).

This book is for those who understand they are in process, but long for a faster spiritual growth. The concepts presented will *not* provide instant Christ likeness however the author and many others have found the principles in this book very helpful in both their understanding of the process and their personal spiritual progress.

It is a book for those who can identify with what John Newton said:

I am not what I ought to be,

I am not what I want to be,

I am not what I hope to be in another world; but still

I am not what I once used to be, and by the grace of God

I am what I am.

I like the way Charles Spurgeon put it: "'You are no saint,' says the devil. Well if I'm not, I am a sinner, and Jesus Christ came into the world to save sinners. Sink or swim, I go to Him; other hope, I have none."

With that being said, the normal, not average, Christian is growing more like Jesus Christ as they continue their life on earth. "But we all, with unveiled face, beholding as in a mirror the glory of the Lord, are being transformed into the same image from glory to glory, just as by the Spirit of the Lord" (2 Corinthians 3:18).

Prolog

You can't change what has happened in your life so far.

It's how you live the rest of your life that you can manage.

What is your definition of success? I once heard a story about a kamikaze pilot. *It seems that it was his 28th mission!* Unfortunately, that is often the story of well-meaning Christians who desire to live a life pleasing to their Lord. *Has that been true for you?*

Some Christians have great desire to live a Godly life but keep falling into a feeling of helplessness. They just don't see a way out of particular habitual sin patterns.

A common contemporary saying is, "The definition of insanity is to keep on doing what you've been doing and expecting a different result." Yet often, because of habits that is how we live our Christian lives.

If you are frustrated with the progress in your Christian life this book is for you. The purpose of this book is to show a clear path for moving forward in our Christian maturity. As the author, I have two primary goals for my readers.

First, a presentation of a clear and straightforward process that enables anyone to become more Christ-like regardless of the environment in which they are living.

Second, do so in such a way as to be meaningful regardless of the level of Christian maturity a reader has already gained.

Success Is Not Final

Success has been defined in literally thousands of ways. In my career as a management consultant I collected definitions of success, most of which came from secular sources. One of my favorites: "You are a success if at your funeral there are six pall-bearers none of which look at their watch."

Many have risen to extreme levels of success only to find it was temporary. This is true in the financial world, in our relationships with other people, and in all the areas of life that one might define as success.

Success Can Be Final

Perhaps everyone would desire to be a success at the end of their life.

Abraham Lincoln showed real insight when he said, "I'd rather lose in a cause that will ultimately succeed, than succeed in one that will ultimately fail."

One of my favorite sayings is, "Don't sacrifice the permanent on the altar of the immediate."

Jesus said, "For what profit is it to a man if he gains the whole world, and loses his own soul? Or what will a man give in exchange for his soul?" (Matthew 16:26).

Final success is possible and will be rewarded when hearing, "Well done, good and faithful servant... enter into the joy of your Lord" (Matthew 25:23).

Failure Is Not Final

From an anonymous writer: Jacob was a cheater, Noah got drunk, Jonah ran from God, Gideon was insecure, Miriam was a gossip, Martha was a worrier, Thomas was a doubter, Sarah was impatient, Elijah was depressed, Moses stuttered, Zacchaeus was short, King David had an affair, Peter had a temper, Paul was a murderer, Abraham was old, and Lazarus was dead. *Now, what's your excuse?*

God doesn't call the qualified—He qualifies the called!

A couple of New Testament examples: Paul went from being a persecutor of the Church to a mighty man of God. Peter went from a denier to one of the most influential early church leaders.

In more recent times we learn that Charles Haddon Spurgeon, "The Prince of Preachers," suffered from depression throughout his life.

God uses broken and imperfect people to accomplish His purposes. Mistakes that make you humble are far better than achievements that make you arrogant! Difficult roads often lead to beautiful destinations.

In the secular world of professional sports Tom Landry, the legendary coach of the Dallas Cowboys stated, "The job of a coach is to get people to do what they don't want to do so they can become what they've always wanted to become."

If you are a Christian, then the Holy Spirit is your coach with similar goals.

"You don't have to be great to get started, but you have to get started to be great."—Les Brown

"You can't go back and change the beginning, but you can start where you are and change the ending." –C.S. Lewis

THINK AND GROW

1. Do you have different definitions of success for various compartments of your life (such as career, family, social, physical, and spiritual)?
2. What is your definition of success when you reach the end of your life?

Chapter 1 ~ Overview

"Grace and peace be multiplied to you in the knowledge of God and of Jesus our Lord, as *His divine power has given to us all things that pertain to life and godliness, through the knowledge of Him who called us by glory and virtue,* by which have been given to us exceedingly great and precious promises, that through these *you may be partakers of the divine nature,* having escaped the corruption that is in the world through lust."

2 Peter 2:1-4

Normal or Average?

In my early years in the Christian community I often heard the terms "carnal Christian" and "spiritual Christian" as descriptors of Christian maturity levels. I also often heard the term "spiritual giant" applied to the super-Christians.

The term *spiritual giant* bothers me a lot. The only spiritual giant in my view is Jesus Christ. Let me explain. The first problem is that this is comparing one Christian to another Christian or grading Christians on a curve. An implication is that God grades on a curve and a clear teaching of Scripture refutes that notion. We are comparing to the average, not the normal.

The second problem is historical. May I suggest to you that overall Christianity is so sub-normal compared to the early Church that if an individual began to act like a New Testament Christian they would be considered abnormal. The crux of the matter is that we are not to be better than the average Christian (comparing ourselves) rather we are to become increasingly Christ-like.

When viewed this way, it becomes more of a realistic description to talk about "pygmy Christians" and Christians who are moving closer to being a normal Christian—that is like their Savior Jesus Christ.

The problem with *spiritual giants* is the term is in comparison to average Christians. When we switch to *spiritual pygmies* the term is in comparison to the standard that we have been given.

Target Reader

This book is geared toward Christians. It is for those who have acknowledged their sinfulness and inability to live a life that pleases God through their own effort. It is for those who realize that they need a Savior and that salvation can be found in no other than Jesus Christ! It is for those who have acknowledged before God their sin and have accepted by faith the salvation that only comes from the Son of God—Jesus Christ!

Discipleship happens when the Bible is applied to life. But what about when society makes it difficult to stand for Christ?

Our local culture, our nation's culture, our world's culture is becoming increasingly anti-Christian! What can we do to strengthen ourselves to live a Godly life in a perverse world? In this book, are presented practical steps for living increasingly more like Christ in today's world!

The Key

You cannot change your past but you can to a large degree determine your future.

Jesus doesn't desire that we be like other Christians. Jesus wants us to imitate Him.

Don't compare yourself to other Christians. Compare yourself to Jesus Christ.

The Pyramid Model

For on-going success these steps are sequential. In this book we look deeper at each of the layers and their dependency on the layers below.

It is vitally important that you realize that who you will be tomorrow begins with what you do today!

At the end of your life will you be able to say, "I'm satisfied." Will you hear your Savior say, "Well done, thou good and faithful servant" (Matthew 25:23)

THINK AND GROW

1. The author distinguishes between an average and a normal Christian. How would you summarize this for a young

believer in one paragraph?

2. Looking back over your life have you focused too much on the past rather than what you can do today and in the future?

3. On your current path will you finish strong?

Chapter 2 ~ Foundation: Decision

"That if you *confess with your mouth* the Lord Jesus and *believe in your heart* that God has raised Him from the dead, *you will be saved*. For with the heart one believes unto righteousness, and with the mouth confession is made unto salvation. For the Scripture says, '*Whoever believes on Him will not be put to shame.*' For there is no distinction between Jew and Greek, for the same Lord over all is rich to all who call upon Him. For 'whoever calls on the name of the Lord shall be saved.'"

Romans 10:9-13

It would be easy to assume that those reading this book already have realized their need of a Savior and have realized that Jesus Christ is the only One who can save them from the penalty of their sin. That is because He paid the price for *your* sin when He died on the Cross.

The Gospel of Jesus Christ is the only story where the hero dies for the villain. Salvation is not a reward for the righteous. It is an available gift for those who understand their guilt! Salvation is a free gift, but even free gifts require you to accept them and open them.

Jesus Christ took your place and paid the price for your sin: death! Because of His perfect life on earth He, and He only, was capable of paying for your sin. His death was on your behalf. Now, if you place your trust in Christ "You stand before God as if you were Christ because Christ stood before God as if He were you." –Charles Haddon Spurgeon

This decision is the absolute foundation of the pyramid. Every other level rests on this level with regard to spiritual life and becoming more Christ like.

This is the most critical decision of your lifetime. No other decision comes close in importance.

If any reader, is not sure of their eternal destiny, that is they are not one hundred percent confident of eternal life in heaven with God then you need to decide that before it is too late. This book will not dwell on the salvation decision—but if you are not sure then turn to the "APPENDIX C – The Simplicity of Salvation" now and settle the issue.

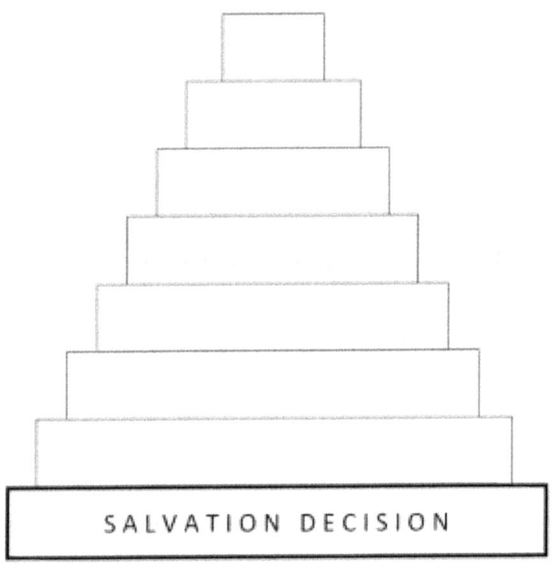

For those who have made this important decision the goal is to climb to the top of this pyramid.

It may not be a continuous climb. At times you might stop and rest. At times you may find that you slip back a level or two. The key is to get up and start climbing again.

The Three Aspects of Salvation

Once a person has made the decision to follow Christ a *process* begins.

At the time of a decision a person can confidently say, "I have been saved!" This is *past* tense. This relates to the *penalty* of sin. It is a time of *justification* before God – not on your merit but on Christ's merit. God, the Father, now sees you covered with Christ's righteousness.

This begins the life-long journey of "I am being saved!" This is present tense and relates to the increasing ability to resist the *power* of sin. The common term for this phase is *sanctification*.

One day the Christian will either die or be raptured when Christ returns. This is *future* and relates to leaving the *presence* of sin. This is the point of *glorification*.

The chart below might be helpful:

Phase One	Phase Two	Phrase Three
Justification	Sanctification	Glorification
Saved from the penalty of sin	Saved from the power of sin	Saved from the presence of sin
Faith	Faith and works	Works
Unbeliever	Believer in time	Believer in eternity

The Sanctification Process

A few years after the major Mt. St. Helens eruption I climbed to the summit with some friends. It was an easy hike until the last hundred yards or so. The ascent at that point consisted of steep coarse ash. Often after taking a step upward we would slide downward most of our step and sometimes even more than our last step!

I have found Christian maturity to be a similar process. The important thing is to keep climbing!

"So what do we do? Keep on sinning so God can keep on forgiving? I should hope not! If we've left the country where sin is sovereign, how can we still live in our old house there" (Romans 6:1-2, msg).

The base level is having personally made the Salvation Decision—a one-time event—by inviting Jesus Christ to come into your life and work through you that which you cannot do by your own effort.

While you cannot change your past, you can change your future!

There is no elevator to spiritual success, you must climb the steps. In order to climb correctly, you must first see the steps, recognize reality, and keep climbing the pyramid.

Remember that it is not about *perfection*. Spiritual perfection will only be achieved when we reach heaven. It is about *progress*. It is about our journey here on earth.

"We cannot become what we want by remaining what we are." –Max Depree

Focus on the next step and not the whole staircase.

THINK AND GROW

Are you positive that you are a Christian? If not, read "Appendix C – The Simplicity of Salvation" now. If you are sure then proceed to the questions below.

    1. Do you understand the three aspects of salvation? If not

consider the following Scripture:

    a. Past (separation from the penalty of sin) – 1 Corinthians 6:11; Titus 3:5; Colossians 1:13-14; Ephesians 2:8; Romans 5:1-2; Colossians 2:1.

    b. Present (separation from the power of sin) – Philippians 1:6; 2:12-13; 2 Peter 3:17-18; Romans 8:29; 2 Corinthians 3:18, 4:16-17.

    c. Future (separation from the presence of sin) – Matthew 10:22; James 1:12; Hebrews 10:39; Revelation 2:1; Philippians 3:20-21; 1 John 3:1-3.

2. How do you feel about your current intimacy with God compared to what you would like it to be?

3. In the past when your busy life has become even busier, which items did you discontinue? *Number them in sequence.*

    a. Personal cleanliness (brushing teeth, bathing / showering)

    b. Eating

    c. Your career / obligations to others

    d. Daily devotions / specific prayer time / Bible study

4. Based upon your understanding of the Bible, how do you feel God would rank the following in order of importance? *(1 = highest, 2 = next, and 3 = last)*

    a. Your service for Him

    b. Your love for Him

    c. Your witness for Him

5. Based upon actual present conditions, how do you rank the following?

    a. Your service for Him

    b. Your love for Him

    c. Your witness for Him

6. Do you think you need any improvements in your communication and intimacy with God?

7. Do you clearly understand the process required to improve your intimacy?

8. What advantages do you think might result from a greater degree of intimacy and a closer walk with God?

Chapter 3 ~ Level 1: Decisions

"Now therefore, fear the Lord, serve Him in sincerity and in truth, and put away the gods which your fathers served on the other side of the River and in Egypt. *Serve the Lord!* And if it seems evil to you to serve the Lord, *choose for yourselves this day whom you will serve,* whether the gods which your fathers served that were on the other side of the River, or the gods of the Amorites, in whose land you dwell. But *as for me and my house, we will serve the Lord.*"

Joshua 24:14-15

There is no elevator to sustained victory. You have to take a step at a time. In this chapters verse immediately above we find "choose for yourselves *this day* whom you will serve." It is not a one-time decision but ongoing daily decisions.

Discipleship Decisions

SALVATION DECISION

In the first chapter we discussed the all-important salvation decision (singular). This is far and away the most important decision any individual can make.

Now we look at the process of on-going everyday decisions (plural) that are necessary if we are to grow increasingly like Jesus Christ. We need to be in the continual state of making good decisions.

It is estimated that we make an average of about 35,000 decisions a day. Many of those are routine such as what time to get up, whether to brush your teeth, etc. But the non-routine decisions are usually the ones to watch out for. These decisions will determine the overall course of your day, your year, and your life!

Salvation is a one-time free decision but discipleship is an-going course of costly decisions.

Discipleship

Throughout the Bible we only find the word "*Christian*" a total of three times while the word "*disciple*" is found over 250 times.

It is one thing to *know about* God and an entirely different thing to *really know* God. A disciple has a deep-seated commitment to God rather than just an intellectual knowledge.

God desires a relationship of close intimacy. Out of that relationship of intimacy comes not only words but action.

"Jesus said to him, "'You shall love the Lord your God with all your heart, with all your soul, and with all your mind." This is the first and great commandment. And the second is like it: "You shall love your neighbor as yourself." On these two commandments hang all the Law and the Prophets'" (Matthew 22:37-40).

"But someone will say, 'You have faith, and I have works.' Show me your faith without your works, and I will show you my faith by my works. You believe that there is one God. You do well. Even the demons believe — and tremble! But do you want to know, O foolish man, that faith without works is dead?" (James 2:18-21).

The important thing which these two passages point out is that while good works have nothing to do with gaining salvation, they are at the heart of a disciple who is growing more Christlike.

Daily Choices

How you live your God given life is your choice, so decide wisely.

Anger is a choice. Revenge is a choice. Resentment is a choice. Negativity is a choice.

Optimism is a choice. Compassion is a choice. Empathy is a choice. Forgiveness is a choice.

Your choices today are the building blocks of who you will be tomorrow.

"Put into practice your Godly convictions. I want you to *beware of letting good thoughts and Godly convictions slip away*, if you have them, cherish them and nourish them, lest you lose them forever. Make the most of them, lest they take to themselves wings and flee away. Have you an inclination to begin praying? Put it in practice at once. Have you an idea of beginning really to serve Christ? Set about it at once. Are you enjoying any spiritual light? See that you live up to your light. Trifle not with opportunities, lest the day come when you will want to use them, and not be able. Linger not, lest you become wise too late." –J.C. Ryle

You Decide Your Ending

Henry Wadsworth Longfellow wrote, "Great is the art of beginning, but greater the art is of ending."

Joshua in the Old Testament said, "Choose for yourselves this day whom you will serve, whether the gods which your fathers served that were on the other side of the River, or the gods of the Amorites, in whose land you dwell. But *as for me and my house, we will serve the Lord*" (Joshua 24:15b).

Jesus in the New Testament said, *"If anyone desires to come after Me, let him deny himself, and take up his cross, and follow Me"* (Matthew 16:24b).

John MacArthur put it this way, "Jesus said, 'If you want to follow Me, you must deny yourself' (Luke 9:23). This is an amazing statement, considering the way people think about the role of Jesus in their lives today. The gospel is not about self-fulfillment, as many suppose. It is about self-denial."

The Apostle Paul understood this, *"I affirm, by the boasting in you which I have in Christ Jesus our Lord, I die daily"* (1 Corinthians 15:31). Paul understood our Lord's command: "Then He said to them all, 'If anyone desires to come after Me, let him deny himself, and take up his cross *daily*, and follow Me'" (Luke 9:23).

Denying oneself is at the very core of true Christianity. It is a matter of putting Christ first in your life.

Note carefully that Jesus Christ never commanded us to take up our cross occasionally, once a week or when we are in the mood. He said, '*Daily*.'

Daily is used here meaning frequently or continually. In truth, to constantly honor Christ we are constantly making decisions according to His desires for us. This often involves multiple specific choices during a day. As we do, we learn about God's desires for us from the Word of God as we are taught by the Spirit of God.

The initial salvation decision was a one-time event – you have been saved from the *penalty* of sin. The Discipleship Decisions are ongoing – you are being saved from the *power* of sin.

Historic Christianity

The Church throughout history has understood this concept. Consider these quotes:

"The first lesson in Christ's school is self-denial." –Matthew Henry

"It is as true of Christians as it is of Christ, there can be no life without death, there can be no sweet without bitter, there can be no crown without a cross. Without Christ's death there would have been no life for the world. Unless we are willing to die to sin and crucify all that is most dear to the flesh and blood, we cannot expect any benefit from Christ's death. Let us remember these things, and take up our cross daily, like men." –J.C. Ryle

"Many obey the gospel so long as it tells them about Christ's part in shedding His blood to save sinners freely. But when the gospel tells them their part, that they must deny themselves, crucify their lusts, and take up the cross, they turn back." –Samuel Rutherford

"The old man [Colossians 3:9-10; Ephesians 4:22-24] is not sent to the hospital to be healed, but to the Cross to be crucified." ... "I have now concentrated all of my prayers into one, that I may die to self, and live wholly to Him." –Charles Haddon Spurgeon

The Way to Intimacy With God

"Now there were certain Greeks among those who came up to worship at the feast. Then they came to Philip, who was from Bethsaida of Galilee, and asked him, saying, 'Sir, *we wish to see Jesus.*' Philip came and told Andrew, and in turn Andrew and Philip told Jesus.

"But Jesus answered them, saying, 'The hour has come that the Son of Man should be glorified. Most assuredly, I say to you, *unless a grain of wheat falls into the ground and dies, it remains alone; but if it dies, it produces much grain.* He who loves his life will lose it, and he who hates his life in this world will keep it for eternal life. If anyone serves Me, let him follow Me; and where I am, there My servant will be also. If anyone serves Me, him My Father will honor" (John 12:20-26).

"Then He said to them all, '*If anyone desires to come after Me, let him deny himself, and take up his cross daily, and follow Me.* For whoever desires to save his life will lose it, but whoever loses his life for My sake will save it. For what profit is it to a man if he gains the whole world, and is himself destroyed or lost? For whoever is ashamed of Me and My words, of him the Son of Man will be ashamed when He comes in His own glory, and in His Father's, and of the holy angels" (Luke 9:23-26).

The Process of Sanctification

The theological term for this process is sanctification. The root concept is to be set apart for God and His kingdom. Christians are citizens of another world (heaven) and that is where their allegiance should be. We are pilgrims passing through a foreign land – however often we act far more like tourists.

Sanctification is the expected process for a believer. "But sanctify the Lord God in your hearts, and always be ready to give a defense to everyone who asks you a reason for the hope that is in you, with meekness and fear; having a good conscience" (1 Peter 3:15-16a).

The Apostle Paul understood this. "I affirm, by the boasting in you which I have in Christ Jesus our Lord, *I die daily*" (1 Corinthians 15:31).

Initial Repentance

Unfortunately, the term repentance is not heard as often in churches today as it was in the past. Often we over simplify the process of initial salvation by making it simply "accept Christ as your Savior," or "repeat the sinner's prayer after me." While those can and often are meaningful phrases the danger is that the person being "saved" has never come to a meaningful understanding of the depth of their sin and the resulting wrath of God upon it.

Years ago, my first sales manager told me something I never forgot. He said that to be successful in sales that you first had to dig a hole, kick your prospect into the hole, make sure they understood the hole they are in, and then show them a ladder out of the hole. It was and is good advice. Most people don't buy something they don't feel a need for.

In salvation the process is quite similar. First a person must recognize their guilt as a sinner, then they need to understand the penalty that God imposes on that sin, once they understand the depth of the hole they are in they are open to receiving information about the only way out of their hole. The ladder out is the Cross of Calvary and their sin debt paid by Jesus Christ. They also need to understand that while the debt has been fully paid they must proactively accept that gift of salvation. While people generally aren't sold that which they see no need for they willingly buy something for which they see a great need.

On-Going Repentance

While the Christian is on earth they continue to sin, hopefully less and less, and therefore they need to continue to repent and ask for God's help as they continue in the process of becoming more Christ-like.

"And so we are transfigured much like the Messiah, our lives gradually becoming brighter and more beautiful as God enters our lives and we become like Him" (2 Corinthians 3:18b msg).

Listen to what some great Christian leaders of the past have said.

John Calvin put it this way, "Repentance is not merely the start of the Christian life it is the Christian life."

Arthur W. Pink said, "The Christian who has stopped repenting has stopped growing."

"Sincere repentance is continual. Believers repent until their dying day. Every other sorrow yields in time, but sorrow for sin grows with our spiritual growth, and it's so sweet a bitterness that we thank God we're permitted to enjoy and suffer it until we enter our eternal rest." –Charles Spurgeon

Paul wrote in his second letter to the Corinthians, "I know I distressed you greatly with my letter. Although I felt awful at the time, I don't feel at all bad now that I see how it turned out. The letter upset you, but only for a while. Now I'm glad — not that you were upset, but that *you were jarred into turning things around. You let the distress bring you to God*, not drive you from Him. [Problems in life can either drive a person towards the Cross or further away from it.] *The result was all gain, no loss.* Distress that drives us to God does that. *It turns us around.* It gets us back in the way of salvation. We never regret that kind of pain. But those who let distress drive them away from God are full of regrets and end up on a deathbed of regrets. And now, isn't it wonderful all the ways in which this distress has goaded you closer to God? You're more alive, more concerned, more sensitive, more reverent, more human, more passionate, more responsible. Looked at from any angle, you've come out of this with purity of heart. And that is what I was hoping for in the first place when I wrote the letter. My primary concern was not for the one who did the wrong or even the one wronged, but for you — that you would realize and act upon the deep, deep ties between us before God. That's what happened — and we felt just great" (2 Corinthians 7:8-13 msg).

Paul Washer comments, "Conversion is not like a flu-shot. 'Oh I did that. I repented. I believed.' The question is my friend; Are you continuing to repent of sin? Are you continuing to believe?' Because He who began a good work in you will finish it. He will finish it."

"Being confident of this very thing, that He who has begun a good work in you will complete it until the day of Jesus Christ" (Philipians1:6).

Thomas Watson put it this way, "Repentance is called 'crucifying the flesh', which is not done on a sudden, but leisurely; it will be doing all our life."

"But the fruit of the Spirit is love, joy, peace, longsuffering, kindness, goodness, faithfulness, gentleness, self-control. Against such there is no law. And *those who are Christ's have crucified the flesh with its passions and desires*. If we live in the Spirit, let us also walk in the Spirit. Let us not become conceited, provoking one another, envying one another" (Galatians 5:22-26).

Intentional Discipleship

Becoming Christ like does not happen without deliberate effort. It is a question of dying daily to your natural desires and instead following the Spirit's direction even though it may be opposite of your natural desires.

Die Daily

George Müller was famous for his faith and the way he ran orphanages in England. Read his account, "There was a day when I died; died to self, my opinions, preferences, tastes, and will; died to the world, its approval, or censure; died to the approval or blame even of my brethren or friends; and since then I have studied only to show myself approved unto God [2 Timothy 2:15]."

The Apostle Paul said, "I affirm, by the boasting in you which I have in Christ Jesus our Lord, *I die daily*" (1 Corinthians 15:31).

Charles Spurgeon, the Prince of Preachers put it this way, "I have now concentrated all of my prayers into one, that I may die to self, and live wholly to Him."

Matthew Henry (1662-1714) said this, "The first lesson in Christ's school is self-denial."

> An anonymous writer wrote: "When you are forgotten and neglected and you don't hurt with the insult, but your heart is happy—that is dying to self.
>
> "When your advice is disregarded, your opinions ridiculed, and you refuse to let anger rise in your heart, and take it all in patient, loving silence—that is dying to self.
>
> "When you lovingly and patiently bear disorder, irregularity, tardiness, and annoyance... and endure it as Jesus endured it—that is dying to self.
>
> "When you never care to refer to yourself in conversation or record your own works, or itch for praise after an accomplishment, when you truly love to be unknown... —that is dying to self.
>
> "When you see your brother or sister prosper and can honestly rejoice with him, and feel no envy even though your needs are greater—that is dying to self.
>
> "When you are content with any food, any offering, any raiment, any climate, or any society—that is dying to self.

"When you can take correction, when you can humbly submit inwardly as well as outwardly, with no rebellion or resentment rising up within your heart—that is dying to self.

In order to live this way "My old nature must be slain, it cannot be mended," said Charles Spurgeon.

The bottom line is that living a life that "dies daily" *leads to life* in contrast to living life according to natural desires which *leads to death*. Also, that person who "dies daily" will not find it hard to die physically when their time arrives.

Your Cross

This is all closely related to "taking up your cross," which in its essence is living a life which is daily surrendered to your Savior – Jesus Christ.

"Then He [Jesus] said to them all, '*If anyone desires to come after Me, let him deny himself, and take up his cross daily, and follow Me.* For whoever desires to save his life will lose it, but whoever loses his life for My sake will save it. For *what profit is it to a man if he gains the whole world, and is himself destroyed or lost?* (Luke 9:23-25).

The Root Issue

When a Christian habitually denies himself and takes up his cross daily they will not have to worry about making good decisions and acting as God would desire.

One of my favorite quotes is by Roy Disney (Walt's brother), "Decision making is easy if your values are clear."

Traditional Christian disciplines are so critical. Bible reading and studying, meaningful prayer (conversation with your adopted Father), and fellowship with other Christians are all so critical. These are the areas of life which develop your deep-seated values.

The Key

It is essential to realize that you are running a race and it is not a sprint but a marathon. The early results are not critical. The aim is to finish well. So always keep your focus on the end-result. Keep your eyes on the finish line.

"Do you not know that those who run in a race all run, but one receives the prize? Run in such a way that you may obtain it. And everyone who competes for the prize is *temperate in all things*. Now they do it to obtain a perishable crown, but we for an imperishable crown. Therefore *I run thus: not with uncertainty*. Thus I fight: not as one who beats the air. But *I discipline my body and bring it into subjection*, lest, when I have preached to others, I myself should become disqualified" (1 Corinthians 9:24-27).

To run a marathon successfully you need to be "temperate in all things" – to think and act in an appropriate training mode at all times. You run "not with uncertainty" but with the assurances of God's promises. You exercise personal "discipline" or self-control. You always keep the end in mind. You keep your eye on the finish line at all times.

It's Up To You

If you want to finish well, it is up to you. The ball is in your court. What are you going to do? God wants every one of us to finish the race strong. But it is entirely your choice.

"Then Jesus turned to the Jews who had claimed to believe in Him. 'If you stick with this, living out what I tell you, you are My disciples for sure. Then you will experience for yourselves the truth, and the truth will free you'" (John 8:31-32, msg).

One day we will all meet our Creator and Judge: "Therefore *we make it our aim*, whether present or absent, *to be well pleasing to Him*. For we must all appear before the judgment seat of Christ, that each one may receive the things done in the body, according to what he has done, whether good or bad." (2 Corinthians 5:9-10).

In the coming Chapters are laid out an easy-to-grasp process to increasing our effectiveness in our current process of sanctification – becoming more and more like our Savior.

There is an old question: How do you eat an elephant. The answer is: one step at a time.

THINK AND GROW

1. As you go about your daily life are you conscious of the reality that you are continually deciding whether to please God or go your own natural, sinful way?
2. Have you considered practicing self-denial in little things in order to build character?
3. Can you give some contemporary examples of "dying daily" to this world and its allures?
4. What factors fight against "dying daily"?
5. How would you describe the benefits of on-going repentance?
6. Do you practice on-going repentance?
    a. If not, why not?
    b. If not, will you start?

Chapter 4 ~ Level 2: Thoughts

"For the weapons of our warfare are not carnal but mighty in God for pulling down strongholds, casting down arguments and every high thing that exalts itself against the knowledge of God, *bringing every thought into captivity to the obedience of Christ.*"

2 Corinthians 10:4-5

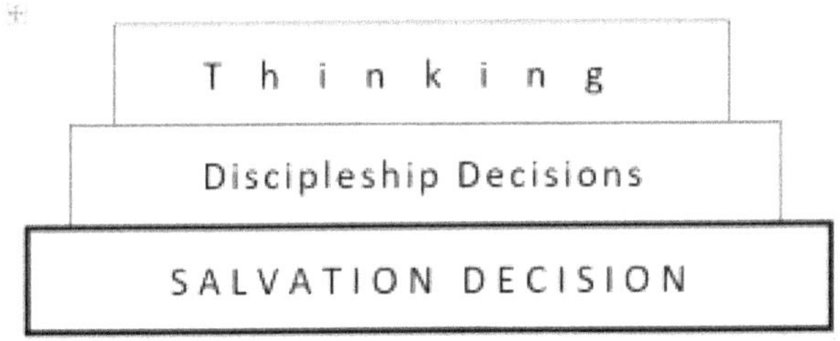

We have previously looked at the Decision of Salvation (singular) which is receiving the free gift of salvation by faith—not by works. Then we moved to issue of the Decisions of Discipleship (plural) which is seeking to live for Christ and the process of becoming more like Christ. Now we look at thinking.

Take Control

Taking deliberate control of your thinking is critical. It is of extreme importance. You will not be able to proceed up the pyramid unless you proactively manage your thought life. Experts say that we have approximately 100,000 thoughts per day.

This is not to be confused with pop-psychology self-talk but rather "bringing every thought into captivity to the obedience of Christ" (2

Corinthians 10:5). Most of what the world tells us about self-talk is very self-centered and egotistical rather than Christ-centered.

"If then you were raised with Christ, seek those things which are above, where Christ is, sitting at the right hand of God. *Set your mind on things above, not on things on the earth.* For you died, and your life is hidden with Christ in God. When Christ who is our life appears, then you also will appear with Him in glory" (Colossians 3:1-4). One of the best ways to improve in this arena is upon waking every morning stop and reflect upon the Cross of Calvary and what Jesus did on your behalf. Spurgeon put it this way, "The more Christ reigns in the heart, the more sin is conquered in the life."

We may move in this direction and soon falter. Satan, our arch enemy then attacks us mentally reminding us of our sinfulness. When he does, we should agree with him and remind him that Christ already paid the penalty of our sin—telling him to get lost!

Satan tries to control, paralyze, and create fear in his targets through their thinking. Jesus calms and advances His people through trust in Him and His goodness.

There is an unseen on-going spiritual battle for us. Our enemy is only attacking us because we're valuable children of God. Remember this, thieves don't break into an empty house. Thieves steal what is valuable. If you were not important to God, Satan wouldn't bother with you!

Someone put it this way: "The devil whispered in my ear, 'You're not strong enough to withstand the storm.' Today I whispered in the devil's ear, 'I am a child of God, a warrior of Christ, I am in the storm but He is with me.'"

Keep in mind that all of God's saints have struggled in their efforts to do this. The Apostle Paul struggled but also gave us the remedy for overcoming.

"For what I am doing, I do not understand. For what I will to do, that I do not practice; but what I hate, that I do. If, then, I do what I will not to do, I agree with the law that it is good. But now, it is no longer I who do it, but sin that dwells in me. For I know that in me (that is, in my flesh) nothing good dwells; for to will is present with me, but how to perform what is good I do not find. For the good that I will to do, I do not do; but the evil I will not to do, that I practice. Now if I do what I will not to do, it is no longer I who do it, but sin that dwells in me. I find then a law, that evil is present with me, the one who wills to do good. For I delight in the law of God according to the inward man. But I see another law in my members, warring against the law of my mind, and bringing me into captivity to the law of sin which is in my members. O wretched man that I am! *Who will deliver me from this body of death? I thank God — through Jesus Christ our Lord!* So then, with the mind I myself serve the law of God, but with the flesh the law of sin" (Romans 7:15-25).

A key point is *don't expect perfection—but seek progress*. Are you more Christ-like today than you were five years ago?

Martin Luther struggled as well: "I sin continually but Christ has died, and forever lives, as my redeemer, priest, advocate, and king."

Root Causes

Beginning at this level of the pyramid we are looking at *root causes* of our behavior. It is not that we should ever expect to follow Christ perfectly in this life. Rather, by understanding the process we will grow more and more like Christ as we finish our time on earth.

If there is any one level of highest importance on the pyramid, it is our thinking. This will become increasingly clear in the coming chapters.

Be careful how you think because your future will be shaped by your thoughts of today. "Keep your heart with all diligence, for out of it spring the issues of life" (Proverbs 4:23). Good thoughts produce good results. Bad thoughts never produce good results. In fact, the heaviest burdens that we carry in this life originate in our thinking.

Secular Leaders

The secular world understands the importance of thinking and thought patterns.

"A man's life is what his thoughts make it."—Marcus Aurelius (121-180)

"A man is what he thinks about all day long." —Ralph Waldo Emerson (1803-1882)

"Change your thoughts, and you will change your world." —Norman Vincent Peale (1898-1993)

"The primary addiction for all humans is addiction to our own way of thinking." —Richard Rohr

Spiritual Leaders

Many Christians have also understood the importance of thinking and thought patterns.

"The battle for personal holiness begins with the battle for the Christian mind." —Steven J. Lawson

"My deepest thoughts will be the material out of which my actions will come." —Earl Radmacher (1931-2014)

"What rules your heart will control your behavior." —Paul Tripp

"Remember that thought is speech before God." —Charles Spurgeon

"The thing that most consumes your thoughts is your god." —Paul Washer

"To be right, we must think right." –A.W. Tozer

"What we think about when we are free to think about what we will—that is what we are or will soon become." –A.W. Tozer

"Our voluntary thoughts not only reveal what we are, they predict what we will become." –A.W. Tozer

"The only way you can be saturated with the thoughts of Christ is to saturate yourself with the Book that is all about Him." —John MacArthur

This last quote is based on the reality that Satan's primary assault is on your thinking. If he can mess up your mind, he will do it. His main *offensive* weapon is lies. Your best *defense* is to fill your mind with the Word of God.

That which controls and dominates your thinking will end up dominating your actions and eventually your life.

Scripture

But what does the Word of God say about thinking? What exactly does God's word have to say about our thought life?

"For as he thinks in his heart, so is he." (Proverbs 23:7).

"And He said, 'What comes out of a man, that defiles a man. For from within, out of the heart of men, proceed evil thoughts, adulteries, fornications, murders, thefts, covetousness, wickedness, deceit, lewdness, an evil eye, blasphemy, pride, foolishness. All these evil things come from within and defile a man'" (Mark 7:20-23).

"For the weapons of our warfare are not carnal but mighty in God for pulling down strongholds, *casting down arguments and every high thing that exalts itself against the knowledge of God, bringing every thought into captivity to the obedience of Christ*" (2 Corinthians 10:4-5).

Importance

Controlling thoughts is a universal issue for mankind. After making a decision to obey Christ's request to "Follow Me" it of most importance to begin a deliberate effort to control our thinking.

The thinking level is where Satan rages his battle! *Satan's primary target is your mind* and his weapons are lies. The antidote is to fill your mind with the Word of God."

If you are not actively checking and controlling your thinking you are headed for real trouble. *Your thoughts will eventually determine your actions.* Long before psychologists started writing about fantasy, the Bible warned of the dangers of our thought life. *Thoughts are the forerunner of action.*

"All of us also lived among them at one time, gratifying the cravings of our sinful nature and following its desires and *thoughts*" (Ephesians 2:3). "But *the mind of sinful man is death, but the mind controlled by the Spirit is life and peace*" (Romans 8:6).

A basic truth to understand is that *your thoughts will eventually produce results.*

The Apostle Paul understood the importance of our thinking: "Now I, Paul, myself am pleading with you by the meekness and gentleness of Christ—who in presence am lowly among you, but being absent am bold toward you. But I beg you that when I am present I may not be bold with that confidence by which I intend to be bold against some, who think of us as if we walked according to the flesh. For though we walk in the flesh, we do not war according to the flesh. For the weapons of our warfare are not carnal but mighty in God for *pulling down strongholds, casting down arguments and every high thing that exalts itself against the knowledge of God, bringing every thought into captivity to the obedience of Christ*, and being ready to punish all disobedience when your obedience is fulfilled" (2 Corinthians 10:1-6).

The Apostle Peter understood this principle: "But Peter said to him, 'Your money perish with you, because *you thought that the gift of God could be purchased with money!* You have neither part nor portion in this matter, for your heart is not right in the sight of God. Repent therefore of this your wickedness, and *pray God if perhaps the thought of your heart may be forgiven you.* For I see that you are *poisoned by bitterness* and bound by iniquity'" (Acts 8:20-23).

The writer of Hebrews understood this principle: "For *the Word of God* is living and powerful, and sharper than any two-edged sword, piercing even to the division of soul and spirit, and of joints and marrow, and *is a discerner of the thoughts and intents of the heart*" (Hebrews 4:12-13).

King Solomon, the wisest man who ever lived, understood this principle: "for *as he thinks in his heart, so is he*" (Proverbs 23:7). *"Be careful how you think; your life is shaped by your thoughts"* (Proverbs 4:23 gnt). *"Be careful what you think, because your thoughts run your life"* (Proverbs 4:23 ncv).

Certainly Jesus Christ understood the importance of thoughts! "Jesus said, 'You have heard that it was said to those of old, "You shall not murder, and whoever murders will be in danger of the judgment." But I say to you that *whoever is angry with his brother without a cause shall be in danger of the judgment.* And whoever says to his brother, "Raca!" shall be in danger of the council. But whoever says, "You fool!" shall be in danger of hell fire'" (Matthew 5:21-22).

Jesus also said, "You have heard that it was said to those of old, 'You shall not commit adultery.' But I say to you that *whoever looks at a woman to lust for her has already committed adultery with her in his heart*" (Matthew 5:27-28). Jesus Christ made it clear that the thought life is absolutely critical.

Why do you suppose Christ, and other leaders, have said such strong words about just thinking about something? It is because our strengths and weaknesses are based on attitudes that have been forming for weeks, months, and even years prior. It is also because *the thinking level is where Satan rages his primary battle!*

If you are not actively testing your thinking and your attitudes, you are headed for real trouble. Before anyone will change what he does, he must first change what he is! Someone has put it this way, "A body is completely dead without a head. That's why Satan attacks our minds first. The body goes where the mind goes."

Thoughts are the forerunners to action. When we allow our minds to dwell on sin, we are programming future sinful actions into our life. The battle is lost at the thought level—before the action decision point!

Sinful Strongholds

Thinking that is left unchecked strengthens until it becomes a stronghold which is increasingly difficult to break.

"Spiritual strongholds begin with a thought. One thought becomes a consideration. A consideration develops into an attitude, which leads then to action. Action repeated becomes a habit, and a habit establishes a 'power base for the enemy,' that is a stronghold." –Elizabeth Elliot

Satan attacks our whole being. Our diet is not only what we eat. It is what we watch, what we listen to, what we read, and the people we regularly associate with. Therefore, we must be vigilant regarding the things we are putting into our bodies emotionally, physically, and spiritually.

Be Christ-like

Speaking of believers the Word of God says, "For whom He foreknew, He also predestined *to be conformed to the image of His Son*" (Romans 8:29a).

"To be conformed to Jesus, we must first begin to think as Jesus did. We need the 'mind of Christ.' We need to value the things He values and despise the things He despises. We need to have the same priorities He has. We need to consider weighty the things He considers weighty." –R.C. Sproul

Evaluation

So how should we evaluate our thoughts? We should evaluate our thoughts by Scripture. The Word of God provides a model, a pattern/template, for our thinking. "Let this mind be in you which was also in Christ Jesus" (Philippians 2:5). Or "*Your attitude should be the same as that of Christ Jesus*" (niv).

"So He said to them, '*Are you thus without understanding also?* Do you not perceive that whatever enters a man from outside cannot defile him, because it does not enter his heart but his stomach, and is eliminated, thus purifying all foods?' And He said, 'What comes out of a man, that defiles a man. For *from within, out of the heart of men, proceed evil thoughts*, adulteries, fornications, murders, thefts, covetousness, wickedness, deceit, lewdness, an evil eye, blasphemy, pride, foolishness. All these evil things come from within and defile a man.'"

Notice a few things about this passage. First, "heart" refers to our human sin nature. Second, "evil thoughts" is the first specific item mentioned. Third, we have a list of typical sinful acts that are the natural consequences of poor thinking.

"As for you, you were dead in your transgressions and sins, in which you used to live when you followed the ways of this world and of the ruler of the kingdom of the air, the spirit who is now at work in those who are disobedient. All of us also lived among them at one time, *gratifying the cravings of our sinful nature and following its desires and thoughts.* Like the rest, we were by nature objects of wrath. But because of his great love for us, God, who is rich in mercy, made us alive with Christ even when we were dead in transgressions" (Ephesians 2:1-5 niv).

"For those who live according to the flesh set their minds on the things of the flesh, but those who live according to the Spirit, the things of the Spirit. For *to be carnally minded is death,* but *to be spiritually minded is life and peace.* Because the carnal mind is enmity against God; for it is not subject to the law of God, nor indeed can be. So then, those who are in the flesh cannot please God" (Romans 8:5-8).

The worst battle you will face as a Christian is the fight that goes on in your mind. And it is a never-ending battle.

The Bottom Line: When we allow our minds to dwell on sin, we are programming future sinful actions into our life.

A Familiar Key Scripture

"I beseech you therefore, brethren, by the mercies of God, that you present your bodies a living sacrifice, holy, acceptable to God, which is your reasonable service. And do not be conformed to this world, but *be transformed by the renewing of your mind,* that you may prove what is that good and acceptable and perfect will of God" (Romans 12:1-2).

The MacArthur Study Bible makes this statement: "That kind of transformation can occur only as the Holy Spirit changes our thinking through consistent study and meditation of Scripture (Psalm 119:11; cf. Colossians 1:28, 3:10, 16; Philippians 4:8). The renewed mind is one saturated with and controlled by the Word of God."

Displacement

What you allow is what will continue. This month's thoughts are next month's thoughts unless you take deliberate action. Even more important today's thoughts will evolve into tomorrow's attitudes – which we explore in the next chapter.

Suppose you had a glass full of milk that was glued to the table and you were instructed to empty it of the milk. You notice a gallon jug full of water. You would pick up the water and pour it into the glass until all the milk was displaced by water.

Now suppose you have a mind full of non-beneficial thoughts that you would like to be rid of. Use this same principle of displacement. Whenever a wrong thought comes to mind deliberately replace it with a good thought. A negative sinful thought can be replaced with a sincere positive prayer to God.

"Brethren, whatever things are true, whatever things are noble, whatever things are just, whatever things are pure, whatever things are lovely, whatever things are of good report, if there is any virtue and if there is anything praiseworthy — meditate on these things" (Philippians 4:8).

Even better be specific and replace your bad thought with an opposite thought. The most effective way to do this is to fill your mind with the Word of God so that you can respond with Scripture relating to the thought you are displacing and replacing. "Your word I have hidden in my heart, that I might not sin against You" (Psalm 119:11).

Consider

Luis Palau wrote in his booklet *Experiencing God's Forgiveness*: "Within the last two years I have learned of several well-known leaders who have fallen into serious sin. I have known one of these men for years. He was an out-going, winsome fellow who preached strongly against sin.

"Then one day he left his family and took up with another woman. He admits making some mistakes, but he blames his wife, he blames the Lord, he blames his friends – everybody but himself."

"How does something like this happen?

"In almost all of cases like these the individual had secretly been filling their mind with wrong thoughts pornography, or other sinful thoughts for years.

"Once thinking is shifted from the things of the Lord, the world quickly offers a subtle but destructive 'thrill' as a substitute."

The Apostle Paul could say in 2 Corinthians 10:5b that he brought *"every thought into captivity to the obedience of Christ."*

"Therefore, holy brothers, who share in the heavenly calling, *fix your thoughts on Jesus*, the Apostle and High Priest whom we confess" (Hebrews 3:1, niv).

Quick Review

Beginning with our thinking each chapter looks at a theme which runs throughout the Bible. What our pyramid shows is that each of these critical themes are inter-related – there is also a hierarchy of how they fit together. It is my belief that by the end of this book each reader will be convinced of the interrelated and generally sequential aspects of these themes.

The *Salvation Decision* (singular) is not a step in the pyramid but rather it is the absolute foundation. The first level of our pyramid climb is *Discipleship Decisions* (plural) which is the starting point for sustained maturing in the Christian life.

We saw that the "*Follow Me*" command of our Lord Jesus Christ is a most basic theme throughout Scripture—that we ought to Follow (or pursue) Christ both for salvation *and* regarding daily living.

I like what Andrew Farley has said, "The goal isn't perfect performance. The goal is knowing Jesus and His perfect performance 2,000 years ago." As we focus on Christ our performance will move closer and closer to perfect performance.

Paul has shown us the way to guard our minds: "*Be anxious for nothing, but in everything by prayer and supplication, with thanksgiving, let your requests be made known to God; and the peace of God, which surpasses all understanding, will guard your hearts and minds through Christ Jesus*" (Philippians 4:6-7).

Notice the dual-responsibility in this passage: "Be anxious for nothing" (guard your minds) – that is our part as part of our responsibility before God. Later, "the peace of God... will guard your hearts and minds" – that is God's part illustrating our dependence upon Him. But Paul continues providing us instruction as he continues in this same passage.

The best defense is a good offense! "Finally, brethren, whatever things are true, whatever things are noble, whatever things are just, whatever things are pure, whatever things are lovely, whatever things are of good report, if there is any virtue and if there is anything praiseworthy—*meditate on these things. The things which you learned and received and heard and saw in me, these do, and the God of peace will be with you*" (Philippians 4:8-9).

We must guard our minds from wrong thoughts because left un-checked they lead to wrong deeds.

"The greatest weapon against stress is our ability to choose one thought over another." —William James

A Meaningful Song

The song "Think on the Good Things" captures this concept very well.

I'm gonna think on the good things!
Think on what the Lord has done for me.
I'm gonna think about the good, good things!
What I think is what I'm gonna be.

I'm gonna fill up my mind with happy songs of praise,
Remind myself that He's forgiven me.
I'm gonna think about the things
That I know will lift me up –
Like hope and peace and truth and love and simple honesty.

I'm gonna think on the good things!
Think on what the Lord has done for me.
I'm gonna think about the good, good things!
What I think is what I'm gonna be.

If I think about despair, I will only get depressed;
If I dwell on trouble, I will troubled be.
But if I fill up my mind with the goodness of the Lord,
He will make me more like Him,
And meet my every need.

I'm gonna think on the good things!
Think on what the Lord has done for me.
I'm gonna think about the good, good things!
What I think is what I'm gonna be.

Lyrics by Gloria Gaither and Gary McSpadden. Music by Bill Gaither and Gary McSpadden.

THINK AND GROW

1. What can we expect if we do not control our thoughts?
    (Romans 8:6a)

2. What can we expect if we do control our thoughts? (Romans 8:6b; Psalm 103:5, 37:4)

3. Are you willing to accept Biblical challenges?
    a. Ephesians 4:23
    b. Romans 12:2

4. Are you willing to enlist the cooperation of the Spirit of God?
    a. To fill your mind (John 6:63; 1 Corinthians 2:12-13a)?
    b. To provide help (Psalm 86:1, 90:14, 119:18, 36)?
    c. To personally work at continual consciousness of His availability?

5. Are you willing to purposely regularly think about what you think about?

Chapter 5 ~ Level 3: Attitudes

"Your attitude should be the same as that of Christ Jesus."

Philippians 2:5, niv

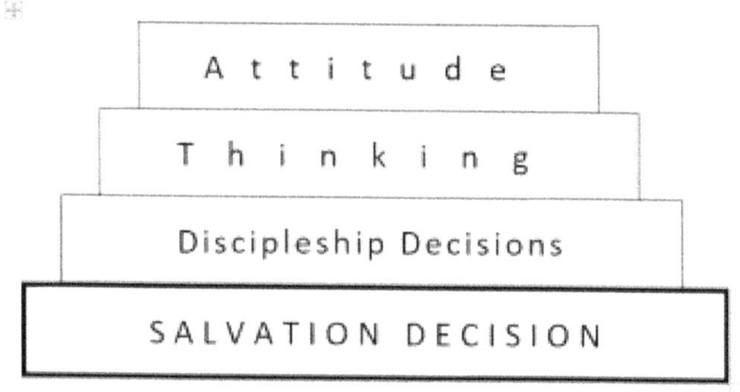

The next step is to deliberately evolve our attitudes (plural). This is closely related, but distinct, from thinking. It is essential that we understand the close relationship of thinking and attitudes.

Take a few minutes to reflect on what comes to your mind when you read each of the following phrases? The Bible... The Salvation Army... The Red Cross... The Post Office... The IRS... Hillary Clinton... Donald Trump... Joe Biden... Jimmy Carter... Ronald Reagan... Chevrolet... Ford... Dodge... Taxation... Congress... Baptists... Presbyterians... Methodists... Christian Scientists... Mormons...

Most people will have a stronger response to some of those items than others. Some responses might be positive while others are negative. Those with a stronger reaction were based on firmly established attitudes.

It is a reality that many of our strengths and weaknesses are influenced by the attitudes we have formed over the weeks, months, and years of the past.

At an early age we begin forming attitudes as we are repeatedly taught certain values or principles. Always clean your plate! Don't talk to strangers! Don't cross against the red light! Always look both ways before crossing. Stop – Look – Listen. Clean your room.

Definition

What is an attitude? The most concise definition I have found is *a habit of thinking*. An attitude is a habit of thought—a habitual thought pattern regarding something specific. The obvious factor that comes to mind is that a thinking pattern can be positive or negative. An attitude can be thought of as a thinking rut.

Thinking ruts can be useful or harmful. It is useful to have a habit of brushing your teeth every morning and because it is a habit you don't have to think each morning whether to take care of personal hygiene. It's handy to know when ordering food in a restaurant whether you like their daily special of liver and onions or not.

Harmful habits are just as common as helpful habits. Think of addictions to harmful substances. Or the issue of socially poor habits such as gossip or always interrupting conversations.

How are attitudes developed? It should be clear that habits come from repetition.

When you repeatedly think in a particular way it will become an *attitude*. Attitudes are insidious. You think a particular way just once. But the next time it is easy to think the way you did the previous time. Before long you have developed an attitude (a habitual way of thinking). That is why it is critical to constantly test the correctness of your thinking.

We may use the term habitude to describe this reality.

Can you change an attitude?

Absolutely, but it is not easy. There are two main ways of changing an attitude.

The first way is to train yourself to think differently through repetition. Since attitudes sometimes have developed over years it will take time to change them. The concept is displacement. Every time the old pattern of thinking emerges you deliberately change your thoughts to the new way you want to think. Over time it becomes easier and easier. As a Christian if you enlist prayer and the Holy Spirit to help the change time can be shortened—sometimes drastically.

The second primary way is by a significant impactful event. Usually these produce significant emotion.

Two less common ways of changing an attitude is through a memorable event or some combination of these three.

Attitudes normally change slowly except when a significant emotional event happens.

Can you change the attitude of a mature person, other than yourself? It is possible, but relatively rare.

Years ago, I read on the front page of our local newspaper that a local judge had sentenced an accused rapist to five years of probation. This was a tragic mistake in my mind. The individual had prior convictions for three murders and seven rapes prior to the current charge. One of those previous rapes was of the sister of a friend of mine. My thoughts toward both the judge and the prisoner were not good. That is a true story.

Now let's imagine that the judge in question had found out a few days prior that his own wife, or daughter, had been raped by someone. Do you suppose he would have determined the same sentence of probation. Personally, I don't think so. That would be an example of a significant impactful event changing the attitude of a judge.

Are Attitudes Important?

Prominent Bible Teacher Charles R. Swindoll has written: "Words can never adequately convey the incredible impact of our attitude toward life. The longer I live the more convinced I become that life is ten percent what happens to us and ninety percent how we respond to it. I believe the single most significant decision I can make on a day-to-day basis is my choice of attitude. It is more important than my past, my education, my bankroll, my successes or failures, fame or pain, what other people think of me or say about me, my circumstances, or my position. Attitude keeps me going or cripples my progress. It alone fuels my fire or assaults my hope. When my attitudes are right, there's no barrier too high, no valley too deep, no dream too extreme, no challenge too great for me."

As noted previously, a great advantage of well-formed attitudes is that you don't have to decide what to do in each situation!

Your attitudes directly affect your quality of life.

An Illustration

There is a story about an event in a very small town in eastern Oregon. In this state drivers—are not allowed to pump their own gas.

It seems that one day a family pulled into town with their car loaded down and pulling a U-Haul trailer. They stopped at the only service station for gas and explained they had bought the old Miller place a few miles out of town. The station attendant warmly welcomed them.

While the attendant was filling their tank, the man asked him, "What kind of people live here?" The attendant replied, "What kind of people live in the town you came from?" The man replied, "That's why we are moving! They're mean, critical, and would steal the shirt off your back." The attendant softly replied, "Yep, the same kind of folks live around here!"

A couple of weeks later another car pulled in with all the family's possessions in tow. They too stopped at the only gas station to buy gas.

Once again, as the attendant was filling their tank, the same question was asked. "What kind of people live here in your town?" The attendants reply was the same. "What kind of people live in the town you came from?" This newcomer replied, "We hated to leave, people were so wonderful, loving, and caring. Well, they would give you the shirt off their back." Once again, the attendant replied, "Yep, the same kind of folks live around here!"

I think this attendant was a pretty savvy guy!

Secular Leaders

Many secular leaders have commented on the importance of our attitudes.

"The greatest discovery of my generation is that human beings can alter their lives by altering their attitudes of mind." –William James (1842-1910)

"Attitude is everything. Change your attitude… change your life!" –Jeff Keller

"A great attitude becomes a great mood, which becomes a great day, which becomes a great year, which becomes a great life." –Zig Ziglar

Scripture

"I beseech you therefore, brethren, by the mercies of God, that you present your bodies a living sacrifice, holy, acceptable to God, which is your reasonable service. And do not be conformed to this world, but *be transformed by the renewing of your mind*, that you may prove what is that good and acceptable and perfect will of God" (Romans 12:1-2). Look at some key components of this passage.

"Living sacrifice" – A sage once remarked, the problem living sacrifices have is they keep crawling off the altar!

"Holy" – In this passage holy refers to being set apart, put at His disposal—it does not mean perfection. It refers to being different, set apart, unique.

"Transformed" – Actually there are three possibilities. First, we can be "*transformed*." Second, we can be "*conformed*" as seen later in this passage. Third, may I suggest the problem with many is they are *deformed* by trying to do both! Jason R. Doll wrote: "Giving God part of you is like having only half a boat on the sea. It might be a boat, but you're going to sink. Put all your faith in Him."

"Renewing of your mind" – Transformation starts in the mind. That is the reality of our lives.

There are many other passages which contain similar thoughts. Here are a few:

"Therefore, *prepare your minds for action*, keep sober in spirit, fix your hope completely on the grace to be brought to you at the revelation of Jesus Christ. As obedient children, *do not be conformed to the former lusts* [strong desires] which were yours in your ignorance, but like the Holy One who called you, be holy yourselves also in all your behavior; because it is written, 'You shall be holy, for I am holy'" (1 Peter 1:13-16 nasu).

"*You were taught*, with regard to your former way of life, to put off your old self, which is being corrupted by its deceitful desires; *to be made new in the attitude of your minds*; and to put on the new self, created to be like God in true righteousness and holiness" (Ephesians 4:22-24, niv).

"Therefore, since Christ suffered in His body, *arm yourselves also with the same attitude*, because he who has suffered in his body is done with sin. As a result, he does not live the rest of his earthly life for evil human desires, but rather for the will of God" (1 Peter 4:1-2, niv).

Quick Review

We know that as Christians one of our primary duties in life is to become more Christ-like. But how? John Stott put it this way, "We must allow the Word of God to confront us, to disturb our security, to undermine our complacency, and to overthrow our patterns of thought and behavior."

From time-to-time we hear of a great leader who has fallen into some grave sin. A very impactful statement which I heard years ago puts it succinctly. "Failure is rarely a blowout, it is nearly always a slow leak."

The battle is easily lost unless you understand that attitudes are formed by patterns of thinking. Our attitudes should be the same as Jesus Christ our model, which obviously begs the question, what were Christ's primary attitudes?

"Your attitude should be the same as that of Christ Jesus: Who, being in very nature God, did not consider equality with God something to be grasped, but made Himself nothing, *taking the very nature of a servant,* being made in human likeness. And being found in appearance as a man, *He humbled Himself* and became obedient to death — even death on a cross!" (Philippians 2:5-8, niv).

We are to *be characterized by humility* which is an attitude or a frame of mind.

Humility is not a matter of being passive, it is right thinking about yourself in relation to God and others.

Regarding your approach to situations, "Whether you think you can or think you can't, you're right." —Henry Ford

THINK AND GROW

1. Has this chapter caused you greater understanding of what attitudes are?
2. Has this chapter given you a greater appreciation for the importance of attitudes?
3. Do you understand the concept of attitude change through displacement and replacement?
4. Are there some attitudes which you need to change?
    a. If so, list a maximum of two which you plan on changing.

Chapter 6 ~ Level 4: Motivations

"Let this mind be in you which was also in Christ Jesus [think like Christ thinks], who, being in the form of God, did not consider it robbery to be equal with God, but made Himself of no reputation, taking the form of a bondservant, and coming in the likeness of men. And being found in appearance as a man, He humbled Himself and became obedient to the point of death, even the death of the Cross."

Philippians 2:5-8

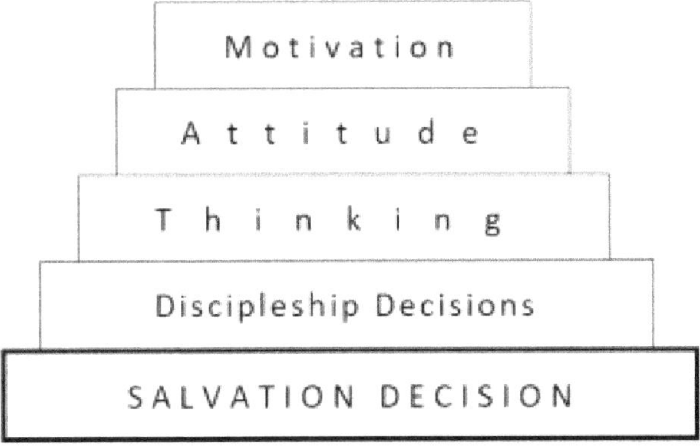

A once heard about a farmer who asked his neighbor if he might borrow a rope. "Sorry," said the neighbor, "I'm using my rope to tie up my milk."

"Rope can't tie up milk."

"I know" replied the neighbor, but when a man doesn't want to do something, one reason is as good as another."

While that story may make us chuckle there is a wealth of truth in it. If you listen carefully as you live life you will hear many excuses for inaction that are just as unrelated to the issue as the farmer's excuse.

The obvious questions are: Why do you do what you do? What motivates you?

Define Motivation

The simplest way, and an easy way to remember, what motivation is by dividing the word: motiv-ation which leads us to *motive-action*. Your reason (motive) for what you do (action) is a simple but accurate way of defining motivation.

An Old Story

Consider this story which I have seen circulating in various versions for decades:

There was a hard-working Christian couple who skimped and saved to send their only child, a daughter—Barbara, away to a fine Christian college. One day they received the following letter:

"Dear Mom & Dad,

"I met this neat guy a couple of months ago. He doesn't go to school, in fact he dropped out of high school! He's trying to find a job, but he has no work experience of any kind—nor does he know what to do with his life. But the important thing is that we really love one another. Mom, Dad, I know you won't approve ... but I've been living with him, my grades have dropped real low, and I'm pregnant! I think I'm going to withdraw from all my classes to avoid receiving failing grades!"

(The tear-struck couple turned to the second page as best they could with their trembling hands.)

The letter continued...

> "Everything you read on the first page is false! However, this term I have dropped from straight A's to a mixture of A's and B's and I do need some extra expense money real bad. Love to you both—as always, Your daughter, Barb."

Now Barbara knew how to motivate her parents by altering her parents attitudes! She motivated them to not be overly upset about her grades and to be willing to help with extra expense money.

Types of Motivation

There are only three broad categories of motivation.

While there are only three primary types, often two or all three types are involved in the same situation. In fact, it is relatively uncommon for only one of the three motivations to be involved.

Personal Protection

A person may detest their career but regularly go to work to avoid some kind of failure or loss.

Regularly going to work in a situation a person hates might be motivated by not wanting to be reprimanded, lose promotion opportunities, lose health benefits, or to avoid being terminated.

In the salvation decision the overriding factor might be to avoid an eternity in hell.

Philip Yancey has written, "Jesus forgave a thief dangling on a cross, knowing full well the thief had converted out of plain fear. That thief would never study the Bible, never attend a synagogue or church, and never make amends to those he had wronged. He simply said, 'Jesus remember me,' and Jesus promised 'Today you will be with me in paradise.' It was another shocking reminder that grace does not depend on what we have done for God but rather what God as done for us."

Personal Profit

In this situation a person's motivation for spending half of his waking hours at work involves some aspect of personal gain.

Even though a person may detest their career they regularly go to work to achieve a paycheck. The motivation continues with the paycheck being a source of gain in what the person can buy or achieve with the paycheck.

In a salvation decision the overriding factor is sometimes to gain access to heaven.

Personal Pride

This category involves the inner self including our value system made up of attitudes, beliefs, self-respect, and consistency of character.

In the work example, this may be more clearly seen with someone who really loves their job. This could be permanent or temporary. One might be on a particular short-term project that they love to the point where they hate to leave work in the afternoon and are anxious to get to work in the morning because of the self-fulfillment they receive from their work.

In the salvation decision the overriding factor maybe understanding God's great love for us and the fact that He was willing to sacrifice His only begotten Son on the Cross for us. This is the believer who is driven most strongly by the verse in 1 John, "We love Him because He first loved us" (1 John 4:19).

As we can see a person might be motivated to go to work everyday because of one, two, or all three of the motivation types. In a similar way a person may make the Salvation Decision because of one, two, or all three of the motivation types.

Summary of Motivation

Consider the following chart of the three motivation types:

Motivation	Personal Protection	Personal Profit	Personal Pride
Alternate Name	Fear	Incentive	Attitude
Symbol	"Stick"	"Carrot"	"Heart"
Source	External	External	Internal
Driving Factor	Avoid a loss or punishment	Gain something or an award	A response from within
Permanence	Temporary	Temporary	Semi-Permanent

Paul Bane has said, "If punishment is the motivation I may change for the moment, but if love is the motivation I may change forever."

Scripture

In a very real sense The Law in the Old Testament was a motivation based on *Personal Protection* (Fear) and *Personal Profit* (Incentive). "If you obey blessing, if you disobey punishment" (for example Deuteronomy 11:22-28). In a large degree the Old Testament saints were primarily motivated by the choice between Personal Protection and Personal Profit.

In our day New Testament believers should be primarily motivated by *Personal Pride* (Attitude).

This can be seen quite clearly in a single passage which illustrates the difference between the Old Testament times and the New Testament era: Hebrews 12:18-23. We will leave this for your personal study. By background...

12:1-2 is about our Race of Faith on earth – looking unto Jesus as our example!

12:3-11 gives us the example of the discipline of Jesus Christ – our example!

12:12-17 is about renewing the vitality of our Christian faith.

In 12:18-21 we see the examples of Old Testament saints (see below).

In 12:22-29 we see the pattern of New Testament believers (see below).

Old Testament

"Unlike your ancestors, you didn't come to Mount Sinai — all that volcanic blaze and earthshaking rumble — to hear God speak. *The earsplitting words and soul-shaking message terrified them* and they begged him to stop. When they heard the words — 'If an animal touches the Mountain, it's as good as dead' — *they were afraid to move. Even Moses was terrified.*" ... (Hebrews 12:18-21 msg).

New Testament

... "No, *that's not your experience at all.* You've come to Mount Zion, the city where the living God resides. The invisible Jerusalem is populated by throngs of festive angels and Christian citizens. It is the city where God is Judge, with judgments that make us just. You've come to Jesus, who presents us with *a new covenant, a fresh charter from God.* He is the Mediator of this covenant. The murder of Jesus, unlike Abel's — a homicide that cried out for vengeance — *became a proclamation of grace*" (Hebrews 12:22-23 msg).

Summary

The contrast of Law in the Old Testament versus Grace in the New Testament can be seen as largely a change in motivations from Personal Protection (fear) and Personal Profit (incentive) in the Old Testament compared to the New Testament where the proper response is an internal heart and life changing response to His love.

"True faith works by love. It constrains a man to live unto the Lord from a deep sense of gratitude for redemption. It makes him feel that he can never do too much – for Him who died for him." —J.C. Ryle (*Holiness*)

THINK AND GROW

1. Have you ever found out that you were wrong regarding what you thought motivated someone else?
2. Can you describe different periods in your life when motivation for your job (including homemakers) was for all three types of motivation?
3. What was your primary motivation type in your personal Salvation Decision?
4. What are your motivation types currently regarding your Christian Life?

Chapter 7 ~ Level 5: Actions

"Finally, brethren, whatever things are true, whatever things are noble, whatever things are just, whatever things are pure, whatever things are lovely, whatever things are of good report, if there is any virtue and if there is anything praiseworthy — meditate on these things. *The things which you learned and received and heard and saw in me, these do*, and the God of peace will be with you."

Philippians 4:8-9

With regular communion with God resulting in regular *Discipleship Decisions* we can train our *Thinking* and develop right *Attitudes* and *Motivations* which will lead to Godly *Actions* on our part. Simple in theory but it is a process which takes time.

Simply said, "Guard your thoughts, and there will be little fear about your actions." —J.C. Ryle

Problem

In modern society we often tend to act, or not act, based upon our feelings. The reality is that if you wait until you feel like doing something there is a strong possibility you will never act. But this is based upon a false premise.

Solution

The reality is that feelings follow behavior! When you act feelings will follow. It is simple to acknowledge this intellectually but because of our inertia it is sometimes very difficult to internalize enough to take action.

We must also realize that everything that we should or must do is not always easy or comfortable. May I say this reverently: if Jesus had waited until He felt like going to the Cross we would still be waiting for salvation. He cried out to His Father:

"Then Jesus came with them to a place called Gethsemane, and said to the disciples, 'Sit here while I go and pray over there.' And He took with Him Peter and the two sons of Zebedee, and *He began to be sorrowful and deeply distressed*. Then He said to them, '*My soul is exceedingly sorrowful*, even to death. Stay here and watch with Me.' He went a little farther and fell on His face, and prayed, saying, '*O My Father, if it is possible, let this cup pass from Me*; nevertheless, not as I will, but as You will'" (Matthew 26:36-39).

While we will never face the problem of paying for the sins of all humans we do encounter required actions which do not sit well with our desires. Consider one example: "Repay no one evil for evil. Have regard for good things in the sight of all men. *If it is possible, as much as depends on you, live peaceably with all men*" (Romans 12:17-18.)

Training

We are all disciplined (or trained) in one way or another! Trained in Godliness or trained in lust, gossip, lying, dishonesty, covetousness, selfishness, etc.

The New Testament has only four passages that specifically speak of training. Three passages are presented in a positive way and the other presents a negative aspect of training.

(1) "Exercise [literally *train*] yourself toward godliness. For bodily exercise profits a little, but godliness is profitable for all things, having promise of the life that now is and of that which is to come" (1 Timothy 4:7b-8).

(2) "For everyone who partakes only of milk is unskilled in the word of righteousness, for he is a babe. But solid food belongs to those who are of full age, that is, those who by reason of use have their senses *exercised* [literally *trained*] to discern both good and evil" (Hebrews 5:13-14).

"Therefore we also, since we are surrounded by so great a cloud of witnesses, let us lay aside every weight, and the sin which so easily ensnares us, and let us run with endurance the race that is set before us, looking unto Jesus, the author and finisher of our faith, who for the joy that was set before Him endured the cross, despising the shame, and has sat down at the right hand of the throne of God" (Hebrews 12:1-2).

(3) "Now no chastening seems to be joyful for the present, but painful; nevertheless, afterward it *yields the peaceable fruit of righteousness to those who have been trained by it*" (Hebrews 12:11).

(4) The other time the word is used in a negative connotation. The passage refers to false teachers, but the principle applies to all of us: "But these, like natural brute beasts made to be caught and destroyed, speak evil of the things they do not understand, and will utterly perish in their own corruption, and will receive the wages of unrighteousness, as those who count it pleasure to carouse in the daytime. They are

spots and blemishes, carousing in their own deceptions while they feast with you, having eyes full of adultery and that cannot cease from sin, enticing unstable souls. *They have a heart trained in covetous practices,* and are accursed children. They have forsaken the right way and gone astray, following the way of Balaam the son of Beor, who loved the wages of unrighteousness; but he was rebuked for his iniquity: a dumb donkey speaking with a man's voice restrained the madness of the prophet. These are wells without water, clouds carried by a tempest, for whom is reserved the blackness of darkness forever" (2 Peter 2:12-17).

This last sobering passage is basically saying "hearts trained in covetous practices" or "hearts trained in greed." Literally "experts in sin."

Spiritual Leaders

Many Christians have understood the importance of being proactive in their actions.

"The reason why many fail in battle is because they wait until the hour of battle. The reasons why others succeed is because they have gained their victory on their knees long before the battle came. Anticipate your battles; fight them on your knees before temptation comes, and you will always have victory." –R.A. Torrey

"What does 'walking by faith' signify? It means that our thoughts are formed, our actions regulated, our lives molded by the Holy Scriptures, for 'faith cometh by hearing, and hearing by the Word of God' (Romans 10:17). It is from the Word of Truth, and that alone, that we can learn what is God's relation to this world." –Arthur W. Pink

"I don't always feel His presence. But God's promises do not depend upon my feelings; they rest upon His integrity." –R.C. Sproul

"To feel God's love is very precious, but to believe in it when you do not feel it, is the noblest." –Charles H. Spurgeon

"There is nothing so deluding as feelings. Christians cannot live by feelings. Let me further tell you that these feelings are the work of Satan, for they are not right feelings. What right have you to set up feelings against the Word of Christ?" –Charles H. Spurgeon

"Christian, beware of thinking lightly of sin. Take heed in case you fall little by little." –Charles H. Spurgeon

Miscellaneous Quotes

"A journey of a thousand miles begins with a single step."

"Many times you will discover that right actions lead to right feelings."

"You can't go back and change the beginning, but you can start where you are and change the ending."

"Never go back to something you had to pray your way out of!"

THINK AND GROW

1. Throughout your spiritual life have you considered your spiritual training as important as your physical conditioning?
2. The author says that we often wait until we feel good about an action before doing it. What are your thoughts about the concept that feelings follow actions?
3. Looking back on your life can you identify a time when you didn't feel like doing something but went ahead and did it anyway and in the process felt good about it?
4. Are you willing in the future to act when appropriate and let your feelings come as a consequence for your actions rather than a reason for your actions?

Chapter 8 ~ Level 6: Lifestyle

"Not that I have already attained, or am already perfected; but I press on, that I may lay hold of that for which Christ Jesus has also laid hold of me. Brethren, I do not count myself to have apprehended; but *one thing I do*, forgetting those things which are behind and reaching forward to those things which are ahead, *I press toward the goal for the prize of the upward call of God in Christ Jesus*. Therefore let us, as many as are mature, have this mind; and if in anything you think otherwise, God will reveal even this to you. Nevertheless, to the degree that we have already attained, let us walk by the same rule, let us be of the same mind."

Philippians 3:12-16

A preacher told this story: "One day I asked the Lord, 'what's a million *years* to You?'" God said, 'it's only a *second* in time to Me, son.' So then

I asked, 'what's a million *dollars* to You?' God said, 'it's only a *penny* to Me, son!'

"So then I said, 'Okay Lord, how about you just give me a million dollars?' God replied. 'Sure son, but you'll just have to wait a second.'"

What are your goals in life? Is it to gain a million dollars? Is it to become more Christ-like?

People who study lifestyles have often said you can understand a person's true motivations by looking at their checkbooks (or credit card statements). What would a careful examination of your spending habits reveal?

The aim of the pyramid is to move from the initial Salvation Decision (free from the *penalty* of sin) to a regular pattern of making correct Discipleship Decisions (more and more free from the *power* of sin). We have looked at a number of key progressive steps to move us to the final goal of hearing our Savior say to us, "Well done, you good and faithful servant of mine" (Matthew 25:20-23).

Many have described the Christian life as a marathon rather than a sprint. That is correct. The goal is to finish strong.

The apostle Paul said, "One thing I do, forgetting those things which are behind and reaching forward to those things which are ahead, I press toward the goal for the prize of the upward call of God in Christ Jesus" (Philippians 3:13b-14).

Some Quotes

"You'll never see the great things ahead of you if you keep looking at the bad things behind you. Look straight ahead."

"Rivers never go in reverse. So try to live like a river. Forget your past and focus on your future. Always be positive."

"God does not want you to try harder, He wants you to trust Him deeper. Stop trying. Start trusting. This will change everything in you."

"He foresaw my every fall, my every sin, my every backsliding; yet, nevertheless, fixed His heart upon me. Oh, how the realization of this should bow me in wonder and worship before Him." —Arthur W. Pink

"Being a Christian isn't for sissies. It takes a real man to live for God – a lot more than to live for the devil." —Johnny Cash

"If God gives you a few more years, remember, it is not yours. Your time must honor God, your home must honor God, your activity must honor God, and everything you do must honor God." —A.W. Tozer

Regardless of Your Age

It doesn't matter what your physical or spiritual age is regarding the future. The decision to make the most of your remaining time on earth is critical.

The key passage for this book is 2 Peter 1:2-4. "Grace and peace be multiplied to you in the knowledge of God and of Jesus our Lord, as *His divine power has given to us all things that pertain to life and godliness, through the knowledge of Him who called us by glory and virtue*, by which have been given to us exceedingly great and precious promises, that through these you may be partakers of the divine nature, having escaped the corruption that is in the world through lust."

This passage is true for all ages. Our enemy tries to distract us in our youth, but he does not stop there. He continues to try to move our attention away from Jesus Christ towards temporal things on earth. The great spiritual battle is largely won by keeping our focus on eternal things.

I don't know who said it, but contemplate this: The treadmill of life is functioning at an ever increasing speed.

We are going to be what we are now becoming! What we are currently working on, *or ignoring*, is the tapestry of our future.

Fortunately, we are never too old to change.

The Pyramid

This Pyramid, when consistently climbed, results in a changed lifestyle. The model is linear, however we often have to regain steps we have temporarily lost.

On one hand it is progressive, but on the other hand it requires constant attention. We must keep on recognizing our responsibility before God—and our dependence on His Spirit. We must continually control our thinking since our attitudes are constantly being formed. Life provides ongoing situations which test our motivations, and so forth. But self-control and spiritual victory are possible.

This Pyramid climb is a never-ending process!

What this book is really about is *true discipleship* in an often fake-world and even fake-Christianity. True disciples are continually and faithfully following their Lord and Savior Jesus Christ.

I do *not* know of any subject that is more important to 21st Century Christians! Shallow Christianity has become the accepted norm for many. However, authentic Christianity is the source of true freedom and happiness.

"Then Jesus said to those Jews who believed Him, 'If you abide in My word, you are My disciples indeed. And you shall *know the truth, and the truth shall make you free*'" (John 8:31).

"Most assuredly, I say to you, a servant is not greater than his master; nor is he who is sent greater than he who sent him. *If you know these things, blessed are you if you do them*" (John 13:16-17).

Nothing Good Comes Easily

As the apostle Paul said when he was strengthening and encouraging the church, "And when they had preached the gospel to that city and made many disciples, they returned to Lystra, Iconium, and Antioch, strengthening the souls of the disciples, exhorting them to continue in the faith, and saying, '*We must through many tribulations enter the kingdom of God*'" (Acts 14:21-22).

"These things I have spoken to you, that in Me you may have peace. *In the world you will have tribulation; but be of good cheer*, I have overcome the world." (John 16:33).

The Prince of Preaches put it this way, "The road of sorrow is the road to heaven, but there are wells of refreshing water along the way." —Charles H. Spurgeon

And Thomas Watson said, "Afflictions add to the saints' glory. The more the diamond is cut, the more it sparkles; the heavier the saints' cross is, the heavier will be their crown."

Arthur W. Pink offered a very practical suggestion, "Cultivate the holy habit of seeing the hand of God in everything that happens to you." Indeed, God is sovereign!

"And we know that *all things* work together for good to those who love God, to those who are the called according to His purpose" (Romans 8:28).

Another Look at the Process

First, it's intention, then it's a behavior, then a habit, then a practice, then a second nature. Then it is simply who you are." —Brendon Burchard

Satan's Tools

Someone has rightly said, "Satan's primary tool is *not* an active sinner, but rather an inactive saint!"

Someone else has put it this way, "To some Christianity is like...

- a *spare tire* (used only in emergencies)
- a *wheelbarrow* (easily upset and must be pushed)
- a *bus* (riding it only when headed their way)

But Christianity should be like...

- a *pacemaker* (something you rely on constantly)

Life is God's gift to us, but also our gift to Him.

Summary Scripture

"Not that I have already attained, or am already perfected; but *I press on, that I may lay hold of that for which Christ Jesus has also laid hold of me.* Brethren, I do not count myself to have apprehended; but one thing I do, *forgetting those things which are behind and reaching forward* to those things which are ahead, *I press toward the goal* for the prize of the upward call of God in Christ Jesus. *Therefore let us, as many as are mature, have this mind*; and if in anything you think otherwise, God will reveal even this to you" (Philippians 3:12-15).

THINK AND GROW

1. On a scale of 1-10 (10 being very good) how do you think

God would rank your lifestyle today?
2. If the rating is less than you desire, which step of the pyramid do you think needs the most work?
3. Are you prepared for the spiritual battle of which you are a key part?
4. Are you constantly alert (see 1 Peter 5:8)?
5. Are you fully engaged in the battle?

Chapter 9 ~ Level 7: Finish Strong

"Therefore we also, since we are surrounded by so great a cloud of witnesses, *let us lay aside every weight, and the sin which so easily ensnares us, and let us run with endurance the race* that is set before us, looking unto Jesus, the author and finisher of our faith, who for the joy that was set before Him endured the cross, despising the shame, and has sat down at the right hand of the throne of God."

Hebrews 12:1-2

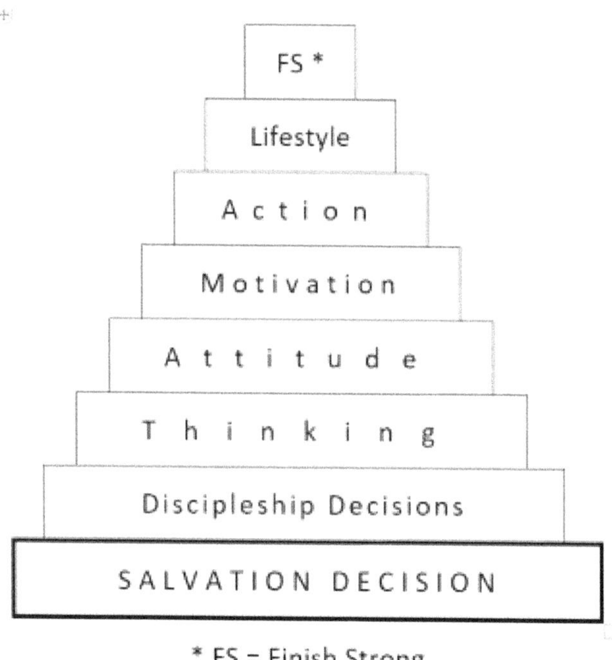

* FS = Finish Strong

"Look not how the Christian begins – but how he ends." —William Gurnall

One of the most humorous epitaphs I have heard about was the gravestone with the name and dates followed by "I told you I was sick."

You *didn't choose* how you came into this world! You are *right now choosing* how you'll come into the next world!

Our enemy does not accept defeat until he has destroyed his foes. As Christians we must not accept defeat until we are victorious in Jesus Christ.

As Christians we don't fear death. Our Savior has conquered death. But what would be the most meaningful epitaph on your grave?

Sobering Questions

If God called you home today, would you be able to say: "I'm satisfied."

If God called you home today, would you expect to hear: "Well done, thou good and faithful servant"? (Matthew 25:21)

It is extremely wise to imagine how we are going to finish this life! How will we be remembered? What did we stand for? What did we stand against? What did we accomplish for eternity?

We need a clear vision of the end, otherwise it is nearly impossible to finish well! We need to focus our life strategy!

"O Christians, would you be happy? Be much in prayer. Would you be victorious? Be much in prayer." —Charles Spurgeon

How are you living your life today? What is your guiding principle?

Caution: Danger Ahead

Many new Christians are very alert and stay close to their newly found Lord. After awhile it becomes easy to become a little complacent, then even careless. We set ourselves up for a spiritual fall without recognizing our danger. We allow vulnerability to evil in our lives. This can easily continue throughout our lifetime.

Many of the great heroes of the Bible faced their greatest temptations near the end of their pilgrimage rather than in the beginning. This true of many Biblical personalities.

For example, Moses, whom God entrusted the Ten Commandments, and the man God used to lead the Israelites through the wilderness when he arrived at the very brink of the Promised Land, lost his temper with the Israelites. He disobeyed God, and as a result God didn't allow him to enter the Promised Land.

Another example is King David, the shepherd boy who sang praises to God and the giant killer in the valley of Elah, the warrior, the poet, and the man after God's own heart, fell to his fleshly lust and became an adulterer. Then that sin continued sin's typical downward spiral and he became a murderer.

David's son, Solomon, at one point considered to be the wisest man who had ever lived became a backslider for a period-of-time.

Sometimes the greatest temptations come after a spiritual success. The point is that no matter what level of intimacy you have with God, be careful. In fact, the closer you are to God the more that Satan will seek to devour and destroy.

The Christian race is not a sprint but a marathon. Sometimes we see marathon runners running a good race only to collapse a short distance from the finish line. They were so close! It was not just about starting well, continuing well, but also about finishing well!

"So I run with purpose in every step. I am not just shadowboxing. *I discipline my body like an athlete, training it to do what it should"* (1 Corinthians 9:26-27a nlt).

"Therefore do not cast away your confidence, which has great reward. For *you have need of endurance*, so that after you have done the will of God, you may receive the promise: 'For yet a little while, and He who is coming will come and will not tarry. Now *the just shall live by faith*; but if anyone draws back, My soul has no pleasure in him'" (Hebrews 10:35-38).

Good News: God Expects You To Finish Strong

There are some Scripture passages which I especially appreciate as I age. They indicate the normal (not average) for a Christian is to Finish Strong.

My pastor has a favorite "senior verse" which he loves to remind seniors of. "The righteous man will flourish like the palm tree, he will grow like a cedar in Lebanon. Planted in the house of the Lord, they will flourish in the courts of our God. *They will still yield fruit in old age; they shall be full of sap and very green*" (Psalm 92:12-14 nasu).

My personal favorite "senior verse" is the well-known passage of Isaiah 40:30-31, "Even the *youths shall faint and be weary*, and the young men shall utterly fall, but those who wait on the Lord shall renew their strength; they shall mount up with *wings like eagles*, they shall *run and not be weary*, they shall *walk and not faint.*"

Why do I like that verse so much? It's the progression in the passage. First, we see even the youth are subject to tiredness and fainting. Second, we have young men falling. Third comes the description of those who maintain intimacy with their Savior. This is where I see great encouragement.

The progression is from *flying* like an eagle, to *running* without tiring, and finally *walking* without fainting. As the child of God grows physically older they may not be as physically capable as they once were but they should be spiritually strong.

"But we all, with unveiled face, beholding as in a mirror the glory of the Lord, are being transformed into the same image from glory to glory, just as by the Spirit of the Lord" (2 Corinthians 3:18).

Great News

Matthew Henry said, "To the wicked man death is the end of all joys but to a Godly man it is the end of all griefs."

No matter what is in your past... No matter where you are now... You can choose to finish strong!

"You can't go back and change the beginning, but you can start where you are and change the ending." —C.S. Lewis

Who you are tomorrow, begins with what you do today!

Satan knows, if he can contaminate your *present* with your *past*, it will forgo your *future* fruitfulness.

C.S. Lewis wrote, "Men have been helped to live by remembering that they must die." And C.H. Spurgeon adds, "Unless we purposely live with a view to the next world, we cannot make much of our present existence."

Scripture

"Do you not know that those who run in a race all run, but one receives the prize? *Run in such a way that you may obtain it*. And everyone who competes for the prize is temperate in all things. Now they do it to obtain a perishable crown, but we for an imperishable crown" (1 Corinthians 9:24-25).

"Therefore we also, since we are surrounded by so great a cloud of witnesses, *let us lay aside every weight, and the sin which so easily ensnares us, and let us run with endurance the race* that is set before us, looking unto Jesus, the author and finisher of our faith, who for the joy that was set before Him endured the cross, despising the shame, and has sat down at the right hand of the throne of God" (Hebrews 12:1-2).

The Three Little Pigs

Jesus Christ is in essence telling us that in the soon coming Judgment Day He is going to blow away our worthless works.

"For we are God's fellow workers; you are God's field, you are God's building. According to the grace of God which was given to me, as a wise master builder I have laid the foundation, and another builds on it. But let each one take heed how he builds on it. For no other foundation can anyone lay than that which is laid, which is Jesus Christ. *Now if anyone builds on this foundation with gold, silver, precious stones, wood, hay, straw, each one's work will become clear; for the Day will declare it, because it will be revealed by fire; and the fire will test each one's work, of what sort it is.* If anyone's work which he has built on it endures, he will receive a reward. If anyone's work is burned, he will *suffer loss*; but he himself will be saved, yet so as through fire. Do you not know that you are the temple of God and that the Spirit of God dwells in you? If anyone defiles the temple of God, God will destroy him. For the temple of God is holy, which temple you are" (1 Corinthians 3:9-17).

Keep in mind that in this passage, which is clearly directed at believers, gold, silver, precious stones represent inward qualities. Wood, hay, stubble represent outward show. This is not just a New Testament concept.

"Therefore, as the *fire devours the stubble, and the flame consumes the chaff,* so their root will be as rottenness, and their blossom will ascend like dust; because they have rejected the law of the Lord of hosts, and despised the word of the Holy One of Israel" (Isaiah 5:24).

Gold represents deity. Gold was overlaid on wood in the Old Testament – Christ's humanity and deity – relationship to God.

Silver represents atonement and redemption.

Hay appears to represent social and welfare services.

Stones represent building – we are called "lively stones."

Stubble is all about activities and works done in the flesh.

Consider the following chart:

Differentiation	*Wood, Hay, Stubble*	*Gold, Silver, Precious Stones* (Temple)
Cost...	Inexpensive	Expensive
Availability...	Common place	Relatively rare
Source...	Easily produced by man	More difficult to produce
Durability...	Somewhat temporary	Long lasting
Construction...	Quick and easy construction	Slow work
Combustibility...	Easily burned	Cannot be easily destroyed
Weight...	Relatively light	More dense

Abraham's Example

I want to be like Abraham. Scripture tells us that he finished well. Abraham died satisfied with his life.

"These are all the years of Abraham's life that he lived, one hundred and seventy-five years. Abraham breathed his last *and died in a ripe old age, an old man and satisfied with life*; and he was gathered to his people" (Genesis 25:7-8 nasu)

"Abraham lived 175 years. Then he took his final breath. *He died happy* at a ripe old age, full of years, and was buried with his family" (Genesis 25:7-8 msg).

Is God Satisfied?

More importantly I want God to be satisfied with my life on earth. But keep this profound thought in mind: "You stand before God as if you were Christ, because Christ stood before God as if He were you." —Charles Haddon Spurgeon

"For since the beginning of the world men have not heard nor perceived by the ear, nor has the eye seen any God besides You, who acts for the one who waits for Him" (Isaiah 64:2).

An Old Hymn:

> This world is not my home
>
> I'm just a passin' through.
>
> My treasures are laid up
>
> Somewhere beyond the blue.
>
> The angels beckon me
>
> From heaven's open door,
>
> And I can't feel at home
>
> In this world anymore.
>
> Oh, Lord, you know
>
> I have no friend like You.
>
> If heaven's not my home

Then, Lord, what will I do?

The angels beckon me

From heaven's open door,

And I can't feel at home

In this world anymore.

THINK AND GROW

It is extremely wise to imagine how we are going to finish this life!

1. How will you be remembered? What will be your legacy?
2. What did you stand for?
3. What did you stand against?
4. What did you accomplish that will count in eternity?

Chapter 10 ~ Nothing New

There is nothing new under the sun."

Ecclesiastes 1:9b

King Solomon understood that there are many reiterations of things, events, and cycles but that fundamentally there is nothing new. What I have laid out in this book is an attempt to put well established patterns into an easy-to-grasp sequence.

Many others throughout time have recognized the sequences that lead to behavior, or more importantly behavior change. In this chapter we will look at some of those to solidify the concepts previously presented.

An unknown author put it this way, "Kind hearts are the gardens, kind thoughts are the roots, kind words are the flowers, kind deeds are the fruits.

Another has stated a progression, "Righteousness in the heart, beauty in the spirit, character in the life, honor in the home, order in the nations, produces in peace in the world."

These demonstrate the importance of understanding and applying the principles of the pyramid.

Elizabeth Elliot has written: "Spiritual strongholds begin with a thought. One thought becomes a consideration. A consideration develops into an attitude, which leads then to action. Action repeated becomes a habit, and a habit establishes a 'power base for the enemy' that is a stronghold."

Steve Larson stated it this way: "There are some Christians who think the mind and the heart are affected by sin, but the will is still free. That is a naive understanding of the human condition that lacks Biblical instruction. The will is simply a handmaiden of the mind and the heart. Wherever the mind thinks and the heart desires, the will chooses."

Now look at a key Scripture passage: Romans 6:1-14:

"What shall we say then? Shall we continue in sin that grace may abound? Certainly not! How shall we who died to sin live any longer in it? Or do you not *know* that as many of us as were baptized into Christ Jesus were baptized into His death? Therefore we were buried with Him through baptism into death, that just as Christ was raised from the dead by the glory of the Father, even so we also should walk in newness of life. For if we have been united together in the likeness of His death, certainly we also shall be in the likeness of His resurrection, *knowing* this, that our old man was crucified with Him, that the body of sin might be done away with, that we should no longer be slaves of sin. For he who has died has been freed from sin. Now if we died with Christ, we believe that we shall also live with Him, *knowing* that Christ, having been raised from the dead, dies no more. Death no longer has dominion over Him. For the death that He died, He died to sin once for all; but the life that He lives, He lives to God..." (vs 1-10).

> This emphasis on knowledge relates to our *thinking*—our thoughts and the resulting understanding.

"...Likewise you also, *reckon* yourselves to be dead indeed to sin, but alive to God in Christ Jesus our Lord..." (v.11).

> In verse 11 the word reckon, or "consider" as some translations state indicates thinking things through carefully (eventually it will turn into an *attitude*).

"Therefore do not let sin reign in your mortal body, that you should obey it in its lusts. And do not present your members as instruments of unrighteousness to sin, but *present yourselves* to God as being alive from the dead, and your members as instruments of righteousness to God" (vs. 12-13).

Now we find the resulting *action* of presenting ourselves (a deliberate decision), to Jesus Christ for His glory.

"For *sin shall not have dominion over you*, for you are not under law but under grace" (v. 14).

Then as a climax to this section of Chapter 6 we find a *lifestyle* (a way of living).

THINK AND GROW

1. While there may not be anything truly new, sometimes we see old things in a new way. Has the material in this book shed new light on information you already possessed?
    a. If so, explain.
2. Have you gained new insights from the material presented so far in this book?
    a. If so, explain.

Chapter 11 ~ Heaven

*"Let not your heart be troubled; you believe in God, believe also in Me.
In My Father's house are many mansions; if it were not so, I would have
told you. I go to prepare a place for you. And if I go and prepare a place
for you, I will come again and receive you to Myself; that where I am,
there you may be also. And where I go you know, and the way you know."*

John 14:1-4

Heaven is beyond human comprehension however we know about
some aspects of our native country and future home.

New Heaven and New Earth

I love to say tongue-in-cheek, "Since God created this incredible earth
in just six-days, imagine what our new home which has already taken
over two thousand years will look like!"

Jesus said, "I go to prepare a place for you. And if I go and prepare
a place for you, I will come again and receive you to Myself" (John
14:2b-3).

"But as it is written: 'Eye has not seen, nor ear heard, nor have entered
into the heart of man the things which God has prepared for those who
love Him'" (1 Corinthians 2:9).

All Things Will Be New

Humans are very vain beings which is part of our built-in pride. Pride
is a root of every sin. Much of our focus is on our outward appearance.
Untold millions of dollars are spent on cosmetics, gym memberships,
and diet plans. While some of this is for health reasons a significant
percentage is purely to make ourselves look better to others!

In heaven all things will be new! It will not be a make-over but entirely new. Yet, at the same time the indications in Scripture are that we will recognize and fellowship with one another! What a great God He is!

We will be like Christ!

There will no longer be competitiveness. No more envy.

New Relationships

On earth I am an introvert. In heaven we will all enjoy a perfect balance of introversion and extroversion! Sometimes when an overly extroverted person gets on my nerves I chuckle to myself knowing that in that future day he or she will be more subdued. And we will all have incredible new abilities and capabilities.

Since Christianity is about relationship rather than religion and the Trinity are all very relational it means we will all be more relational in a perfect sense.

New Activities

God is Creator. In the beginning God created the heaven and the earth. While on earth Jesus created meals for crowds when only a tiny amount of bread and fish was available. Jesus went away, in part, to create our new home. God is a doer. God has promised a New Heaven and a New Earth – one without sin!

We will *not* be sitting on clouds strumming our harps for eternity! Aren't you glad? I believe we will all experience great activities and adventures that suit us. Why would it be any other way?

If you love to travel, God will satisfy your desires. If you love sports, you will be fully involved. If you love to engage in discussion, you will be satisfied. Whatever makes you happy will be available in huge abundance – and for eternity.

Everything Will Make Sense

When my children were young and they came to me with issues or problems I often found myself explaining to them that life on earth is not fair. It is a tough lesson which some of us struggle with our entire lives. As we mature spiritually we realize that we could not expect it to be otherwise in this sin cursed world.

But heaven will be a place where all the unanswered questions and loose ends will make sense. One of my favorite verses in the Bible is, "Now we see in a mirror, dimly, but then face to face. Now I know in part, but *then I shall know just as I also am known*" (1 Corinthians 13:12). In other words, we will know like God knows. I think this means we will be omniscient – all knowing. One of the implications of this is that we won't need to ask any questions or seek any explanations!

C.S. Lewis put it this way, "Our first thought as we enter heaven will be 'Of Course!'"

Fairness At Last

As a young Christian my favorite book of the Bible became Ecclesiastes and I love the way it ends. "Let us hear the conclusion of the whole matter: Fear God and keep His commandments, for this is man's all. For *God will bring every work into judgment, including every secret thing, whether good or evil*" (Ecclesiastes 12:13-14).

The Choice to Follow Christ Will Be Vindicated

We owe the Apostle Paul for so many great truths that he understood, preached, and were later written down for our learning. One of his more startling statements was, "If in this life only we have hope in Christ, we are of all men the most pitiable" (1 Corinthians 15:19). In eternity, the truth of the resurrection and the wisdom of following Christ will be crystal clear.

Organizational Chart

Many Christians believe that everyone will be the same in heaven. There will be no status levels. That is *not* what Scripture teaches. However, there will be no envy or jealousy.

One of my spiritual mentors, Dr. Earl Radmacher, would often say, "Life on earth is preparation time for reigning time." In other words, what we do on earth will determine our position in heaven.

Do not be dismayed because our just and fair God takes all things into account: "For everyone to whom much is given, from him much will be required; and to whom much has been committed, of him they will ask the more" (Luke 12:48b).

The issue is what have you done for eternity with the natural abilities and the spiritual gifts which God has entrusted to you? Some of those spiritual leaders which we highly admire might only be using forty percent of what they have been given. Meanwhile a diligent prayer warrior or a self-sacrificing homemaker might be using seventy-five percent of their gifts.

What we do on earth with what we have been given will determine our position in heaven.

Meanwhile Satan tries to make us focus on the regrets of the past or the concerns and worries we have about the future. God wants you and I to focus on what we can do today and from this day forward for the kingdom of God.

You had no choice in how you entered this world. But you can choose how you enter the next world.

Consider this very relevant Scripture passage: "Then Peter answered and said to Him, 'See, we have left all and followed You. Therefore what shall we have?' So Jesus said to them, 'Assuredly I say to you, that in the regeneration, when the Son of Man sits on the throne of His glory, you who have followed Me will also sit on twelve thrones, judging the twelve tribes of Israel. And everyone who has left houses or brothers or sisters or father or mother or wife or children or lands, for My name's sake, shall receive a hundredfold, and inherit eternal life. But many who are first will be last, and the last first'" (Matthew 19:27-30).

A Time For Rewards

Some Christians are reluctant to talk about rewards and particularly working for rewards – as if that is sinful. But the Bible makes clear that rewards are part of the Christian's future. While it is true, that like anything else, a preoccupation or over-emphasis can become unhealthy and even sinful we must recognize what the Scripture teaches about rewards. That will be the subject of the next chapter.

Think and Grow

1. What part of this chapter stood out to you the most?
    a. Why?
2. Scripture does not give us a lot of details about what heaven will be like. The author points out some general concepts about heaven found in the Bible. Have you taken time to contemplate what heaven may be like?
3. Given what we do know about heaven what are some aspects of heaven that you look forward to?
4. Apparently, there will be levels of status or rank in heaven but without envy or jealousy. Do you find that a difficult concept to grasp?
    a. If so, why do you think that is?

Chapter 12 ~ Rewards

"Look to yourselves, that we do not lose those things we worked for, but that we may receive a full reward."

2 John 8

It is unfortunate that we hear little in most Christian churches and gatherings about rewards in heaven. Perhaps a large part of the reason is the concern that it might lead to unhealthy competition or pride. I believe that Biblical teaching on this important topic leads to integrity and holiness in one's personal life.

"Behold what manner of love the Father has bestowed on us, that we should be called children of God! Therefore the world does not know us, because it did not know Him. Beloved, now we are children of God; and it has not yet been revealed what we shall be, but we know that when He is revealed, we shall be like Him, for we shall see Him as He is. And *everyone who has this hope in Him purifies himself, just as He is pure*" (1 John 3:1-3).

We must understand that God wants obedience and that obedience does matter to God. By our actions we can make God pleased! What a profound thought. When we fully understand that we can bring meaningful delight to the Creator, the God of the universe, we better understand why there will be rewards in heaven for our actions on earth.

The Apostle Paul reminds us, "My beloved brethren, be steadfast, immovable, always abounding in the work of the Lord, *knowing that your labor is not in vain in the Lord*" (1 Corinthians 15:58). In another place in that same epistle Paul writes, "Run in such a way as to get the prize" (1 Corinthians 9:24b, niv).

What we do, as Christians, on earth is important.

Heavenly Rewards Should Motivate

In the Chapter about Motivation one of the three main motivations we saw was to profit or gain in some way. Clearly it would be profitable for any Christian to receive rewards from God.

The Old Testament saints understood there will be rewards in heaven for what we have done on earth. Consider Moses, *"By faith Moses, when he became of age, refused to be called the son of Pharaoh's daughter, choosing rather to suffer affliction with the people of God than to enjoy the passing pleasures of sin, esteeming the reproach of Christ greater riches than the treasures in Egypt; for he looked to the reward"* (Hebrews 11:24-26).

In the New Testament the Apostle Paul wrote, "Who then is Paul, and who is Apollos, but ministers through whom you believed, as the Lord gave to each one? I planted, Apollos watered, but God gave the increase. So then neither he who plants is anything, nor he who waters, but God who gives the increase. Now he who plants and he who waters are one, and *each one will receive his own reward according to his own labor"* (1 Corinthians 3:5-8).

Christ, Himself taught about rewards. "Blessed are you when men hate you, and when they exclude you, and revile you, and cast out your name as evil, for the Son of Man's sake. Rejoice in that day and leap for joy! For *indeed your reward is great in heaven*, for in like manner their fathers did to the prophets" (Luke 6:22-23).

The Prince of Preachers, Charles Haddon Spurgeon, remarked, "There are no crown-bearers in heaven who were not cross-bearers here below." Early in our pyramid we stressed the need to take up our cross daily as we follow Christ.

Rewards of Salvation – Past

At the point of initial salvation we are *justified*. With justification are many benefits, here are a few of those benefits.

Removal of Guilt

"Bless the Lord, O my soul; and all that is within me, bless His holy name! Bless the Lord, O my soul, and forget not all His benefits: Who *forgives all your iniquities*, Who heals all your diseases, Who redeems your life from destruction, Who crowns you with lovingkindness and tender mercies, Who satisfies your mouth with good things, so that your youth is renewed like the eagle's" (Psalm 103:1-5).

"There is therefore now no condemnation to those who are in Christ Jesus, who do not walk according to the flesh, but according to the Spirit. For the law of the Spirit of life in Christ Jesus has *made me free from the law of sin and death.* For what the law could not do in that it was weak through the flesh, God did by sending His own Son in the likeness of sinful flesh, on account of sin: He condemned sin in the flesh, that the righteous requirement of the law might be fulfilled in us who do not walk according to the flesh but according to the Spirit. For those who live according to the flesh set their minds on the things of the flesh, but those who live according to the Spirit, the things of the Spirit. For to be carnally minded is death, but *to be spiritually minded is life and peace"* (Romans 8:1-6).

Our enemy will seek to destroy our effectiveness by reminding us of our past. But Christ has already paid the penalty for *all* our sins. When Satan comes to me with *my past guilt* I like to *remind him of his future*!

A New Creation

"Therefore, *if anyone is in Christ, he is a new creation*; old things have passed away; behold, all things have become new. Now all things are of God, who has reconciled us to Himself through Jesus Christ, and has given us the ministry of reconciliation, that is, that God was in Christ reconciling the world to Himself, not imputing their trespasses to them, and has committed to us the word of reconciliation" (2 Corinthians 5:17-19).

"For in Christ Jesus neither circumcision nor uncircumcision avails anything, but *a new creation*" (Galatians 6:15).

The important thing to understand is that the Christian did not have a "make-over" but is a new man, a new creation. We do have the responsibility of feeding the new man and starving the old nature which is clinging on.

"But you have not so learned Christ, if indeed you have heard Him and have been taught by Him, as the truth is in Jesus: *that you put off, concerning your former conduct, the old man* which grows corrupt according to the deceitful lusts, and *be renewed in the spirit of your mind*, and that you *put on the new man which was created according to God*, in true righteousness and holiness" (Ephesians 4:20-24).

"But now you yourselves are to *put off all these*: anger, wrath, malice, blasphemy, filthy language out of your mouth. Do not lie to one another, since you have *put off the old man with his deeds*, and have *put on the new man who is renewed in knowledge according to the image of Him who created him*, where there is neither Greek nor Jew, circumcised nor uncircumcised, barbarian, Scythian, slave nor free, but Christ is all and in all" (Colossians 3:8-11).

Child and Heir of God

"Now I say that the heir, as long as he is a child, does not differ at all from a slave, though he is master of all, but is under guardians and stewards until the time appointed by the father. Even so we, when we were children, were in bondage under the elements of the world. But when the fullness of the time had come, God sent forth His Son, born of a woman, born under the law, to redeem those who were under the law, *that we might receive the adoption as sons*. And because *you are sons*, God has sent forth the Spirit of His Son into your hearts, crying out, 'Abba, Father!' Therefore you are *no longer a slave but a son, and if a son, then an heir of God through Christ*" (Galatians 4:1-7).

There is a saying in our society, "Like father, like son." That is the goal of the Christian life to become more and more like God.

Received a Down Payment

"For all the promises of God in Him are Yes, and in Him Amen, to the glory of God through us. Now He who establishes us with you in Christ and has anointed us is *God, who also has sealed us and given us the Spirit in our hearts as a guarantee*" (2 Corinthians 1:20-22).

"Now He who has prepared us for this very thing is *God, who also has given us the Spirit as a guarantee*" (2 Corinthians 5:5).

"In Him you also trusted, after you heard the word of truth, the gospel of your salvation; in whom also, having believed, *you were sealed with the Holy Spirit* of promise, who is *the guarantee of our inheritance* until the redemption of the purchased possession, to the praise of His glory" (Ephesians 1:13-14).

What a blessed thing it is to have the indwelling Spirit of God in our lives. Then, to realize that He, the Spirit of God, is proof of the reality of our future forever with God in the New Heavens and New Earth, just boggles the human mind.

Rewards of Salvation – Present

During our ongoing salvation on earth we are being *sanctified*, or set apart, for and to God. With sanctification there are many benefits. Hear some examples.

The Holy Spirit

"And because you are sons, *God has sent forth the Spirit of His Son into your hearts*, crying out, 'Abba, Father!' Therefore you are no longer a slave [to sin] but a son [of God], and if a son, then an heir of God through Christ" (Galatians 4:6-7).

"And do not be drunk with wine, in which is dissipation; but *be filled with the Spirit*, speaking to one another in psalms and hymns and spiritual songs, singing and making melody in your heart to the Lord, giving thanks always for all things to God the Father in the name of our Lord Jesus Christ, submitting to one another in the fear of God" (Ephesians 5:18-21).

What a privilege to have a member of the God head indwelling our lives. He teaches us. He guides us. He convicts and corrects us.

The Peace of God

"*The peace of God, which surpasses all understanding, will guard your hearts and minds* through Christ Jesus" (Philippians 4:5).

"Therefore, as the elect of God, holy and beloved, put on tender mercies, kindness, humility, meekness, longsuffering; bearing with one another, and forgiving one another, if anyone has a complaint against another; even as Christ forgave you, so you also must do. But above all these things put on love, which is the bond of perfection. And *let the peace of God rule in your hearts*, to which also you were called in one body; and be thankful. Let the word of Christ dwell in you richly in all wisdom, teaching and admonishing one another in psalms and hymns and spiritual songs, singing with grace in your hearts to the Lord. And whatever you do in word or deed, do all in the name of the Lord Jesus, giving thanks to God the Father through Him" (Colossians 3:12-17).

If we strive to live according to this passage from Colossians we will have the peace of God within us!

Ambassadors of Jesus Christ

"Take up the whole armor of God, that you may be able to withstand in the evil day, and having done all, to stand. Stand therefore, having girded your waist with truth, having put on the breastplate of righteousness, and having shod your feet with the preparation of the gospel of peace; above all, taking the shield of faith with which you will be able to quench all the fiery darts of the wicked one. And take the helmet of salvation, and the sword of the Spirit, which is the Word of God; praying always with all prayer and supplication in the Spirit, being watchful to this end with all perseverance and supplication for all the saints — and for me, that utterance may be given to me, that I may open my mouth boldly to make known the mystery of the gospel, for which *I am an ambassador* in chains; that in it I may speak boldly, as I ought to speak" (Ephesians 6:13-20).

The Apostle Paul understood that he was a representative, an ambassador, of the King of Kings in a foreign country. In this passage he also laid out the path to victory which is utilizing the tools and protection God has given us to win our spiritual battles on earth.

A Story

Some years ago a teacher in a fifth-grade class asked his students if anyone could explain electricity. One boy raised his hand. The teacher asked, "How would you explain electricity, Jimmy?" Jimmy scratched his head and then replied, "Last night I knew it, but this morning I've forgotten."

The teacher shook his head sadly and said to his class, "What a tragedy. The only person in the world ever to understand electricity, and he's forgotten!"

The point of the story. Some things are not fully understood. The author has written much about the natural phenomena of light – which even today scientists do not fully understand.

When it comes to the Scripture fulfilled Bible prophecy becomes quite clear with hindsight and careful Biblical study. However, an honest observer will admit that future prophecy has been often misinterpreted by the majority. With that in mind, I want the reader to know that the discussion below is the author's best understanding, but not one which he can be dogmatic about.

Rewards of Salvation – Future

One day we will be *glorified*. During our future completed salvation there are still more benefits including the receiving of crowns.

Why Crowns?

Historically, a crown was often the *sign of victory* such as in early Olympic Games. The goal of our pyramid is to finish life on earth victoriously. Late in the New Testament we see this concept regarding crowns (i.e., Revelation 6:2, 14:14).

In recent times crowns are typically a *mark of royalty*. We are right now adopted children of the King of Kings and Lord of Lords. How often as you live your daily life do think of yourself as a prince or princess?

The Bible also notes crowns symbolically as an *honor or reward*. For example, we see honor in the book of Proverbs, "An excellent wife is the crown of her husband" (Proverbs 12:4a). In the New Testament Paul speaks of those whom he had been the means of conversion as his "joy and crown" and as his "crown of rejoicing."

Our focus now regards crowns as a reward for our life on earth.

Crowns in Heaven

Five Crowns or Five Aspects of the Crown of Righteousness

Many Bible scholars list five different types of crowns which will be given as rewards in heaven. Other scholars believe that they may be five different manifestations of a believer's crown in heaven.

Crown of Righteousness

Do you long for Christ's return? If so, there is special reward for you and for all who long for Christ's appearing and being united with Him forever.

Near the end of his life on earth the Apostle Paul wrote, "For I am already being poured out as a drink offering, and the time of my departure is at hand. I have fought the good fight, I have finished the race, I have kept the faith. Finally, there is laid up for me the *crown of righteousness*, which the Lord, the righteous Judge, will give to me on that Day, and *not to me only but also to all who have loved His appearing*" (2 Timothy 4:8).

Crown of Rejoicing

This appears to be for those who have witnessed faithfully of Him, and by their witness have been the instrument through whom others have been won to Him.

"Therefore, my beloved and longed-for brethren, *my joy and crown*, so stand fast in the Lord, beloved" (Philippians 4:1). The Living Bible puts it this way, "Dear brother Christians, I love you and long to see you, for *you are my joy and my reward for my work*. My beloved friends, stay true to the Lord."

"For what is our hope, or joy, or *crown of rejoicing*? Is it not even you in the presence of our Lord Jesus Christ at His coming? For you are our glory and joy" (1 Thessalonians 2:19-20).

Crown of Incorruptibility

Apparently, this crown will be awarded to those who discipline themselves for the daily race so that they might be their best for God and His cause.

"Do you not know that those who run in a race all run, but one receives the prize? Run in such a way that you may obtain it. And everyone who competes for the prize is temperate in all things. Now they do it to obtain a perishable crown, but we for *an imperishable crown*. Therefore I run thus: not with uncertainty. Thus I fight: not as one who beats the air. But I discipline my body and bring it into subjection, lest, when I have preached to others, I myself should become disqualified" (1 Corinthians 9:24-27).

Crown of Life

The crown of life seems to a special reward for those who suffer martyrdom because of their loyalty to God and His Son Jesus Christ (or are willing to if needed?).

"Blessed is the man who endures temptation; for when he has been approved, *he will receive the crown of life* which the Lord has promised to those who love Him" (James 1:12).

In the final book of the Bible Jesus Christ includes the following words to the church in Smyrna.

"I know your works, tribulation, and poverty (but you are rich); and I know the blasphemy of those who say they are Jews and are not, but are a synagogue of Satan. Do not fear any of those things which you are about to suffer. Indeed, the devil is about to throw some of you into prison, that you may be tested, and you will have tribulation ten days. Be faithful until death, and *I will give you the crown of life*" (Revelation 2:9-10).

Crown of Glory

The Crown of Glory awaits those who give themselves to the care of God's flock during the absence of the Chief Shepherd and who do so, without seeking selfish gain.

"The elders who are among you I exhort, I who am a fellow elder and a witness of the sufferings of Christ, and also a partaker of the glory that will be revealed: Shepherd the flock of God which is among you, serving as overseers, not by compulsion but willingly, not for dishonest gain but eagerly; nor as being lords over those entrusted to you, but being examples to the flock; and when the Chief Shepherd appears, *you will receive the crown of glory* that does not fade away" (1 Peter 5:1-4).

Do Not Lose Your Crown!

We are exhorted to beware that no one takes our crown.

Take care how you live. Live in such a way that you do not lose your crown. Jesus' final instructions to the Philadelphian church included this warning, "Because you have kept My command to persevere, I also will keep you from the hour of trial which shall come upon the whole world, to test those who dwell on the earth. Behold, I am coming quickly! *Hold fast what you have, that no one may take your crown.* He who overcomes, I will make him a pillar in the temple of My God, and he shall go out no more. I will write on him the name of My God and the name of the city of My God, the New Jerusalem, which comes down out of heaven from My God. And I will write on him My new name" (Revelation 3:10-12).

Other Crowns In Scripture

Crown of Gold

"Immediately I was in the Spirit; and behold, a throne set in heaven, and One sat on the throne. And He who sat there was like a jasper and a sardius stone in appearance; and there was a rainbow around the throne, in appearance like an emerald. Around the throne were twenty-four thrones, and on the thrones I saw twenty-four elders sitting, clothed in white robes; and *they had crowns of gold on their heads*. And from the throne proceeded lightnings, thunderings, and voices. Seven lamps of fire were burning before the throne, which are the seven Spirits of God.

"Before the throne there was a sea of glass, like crystal. And in the midst of the throne, and around the throne, were four living creatures full of eyes in front and in back. The first living creature was like a lion, the second living creature like a calf, the third living creature had a face like a man, and the fourth living creature was like a flying eagle. The four living creatures, each having six wings, were full of eyes around and within. And they do not rest day or night, saying: 'Holy, holy, holy, Lord God Almighty, Who was and is and is to come!'

"Whenever the living creatures give glory and honor and thanks to Him who sits on the throne, who lives forever and ever, the twenty-four elders fall down before Him who sits on the throne and worship Him who lives forever and ever, and *cast their crowns before the throne*, saying: 'You are worthy, O Lord, to receive glory and honor and power; for You created all things, and by Your will they exist and were created'" (Revelation 4:2-11).

"Then I looked, and behold, a white cloud, and on the cloud sat One like the Son of Man, having *on His head a golden crown*, and in His hand a sharp sickle. And another angel came out of the temple, crying with a loud voice to Him who sat on the cloud, 'Thrust in Your sickle and reap, for the time has come for You to reap, for the harvest of the earth is ripe.' So He who sat on the cloud thrust in His sickle on the earth, and the earth was reaped" (Revelation 14:14-16).

Crown of 12 Stars

"A great sign appeared in heaven: a woman clothed with the sun, and the moon under her feet, and on her head *a crown of twelve stars*" (Revelation 12:1 nasu).

Crown of Thorns

This is the crown which made the other crowns possible!

"Then the soldiers of the governor took Jesus into the Praetorium and gathered the whole garrison around Him. And they stripped Him and put a scarlet robe on Him. *When they had twisted a crown of thorns, they put it on His head*, and a reed in His right hand. And they bowed the knee before Him and mocked Him, saying, 'Hail, King of the Jews!' Then they spat on Him, and took the reed and struck Him on the head. And when they had mocked Him, they took the robe off Him, put His own clothes on Him, and led Him away to be crucified" (Matthew 27:31).

THINK AND GROW

1. At this point in your life which of the past benefits the author listed is most meaningful to you? Why?
2. Of the present rewards which do you currently appreciate the most? Why?
3. As an Ambassador for Christ how would you fair in a

performance review?

    a.   Are some changes indicated? If so, what?

    b.   What are you willing to do about it?

4. Do you think there are five different crowns awaiting believers, or five aspects of one glorious crown?

    a.   Why, or why not?

5. Do you struggle with the idea of working for rewards in heaven?

    a.   If so, why do you think that is?

6. If you died tonight which of the five crowns do you think are waiting you?

Epilog

"His lord said to him, '*Well done, good and faithful servant*; you were faithful over a few things, I will make you ruler over many things. Enter into the joy of your lord.'"

Matthew 25:21

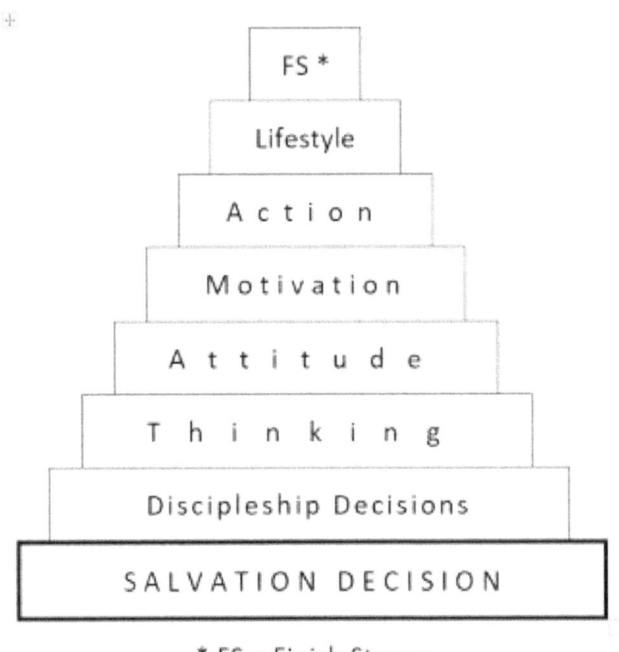

As we start to wrap up this study we must emphasize that it all begins with a choice. This choice requires accepting the fact that you are a sinner, you are guilty before God, the penalty for your sins is death and separation from God. You must understand you cannot save yourself but that God, the Father, sent His Son to pay the penalty of your sins. But you must accept this free gift of salvation. If have not done so, please turn to "Appendix C – The Simplicity of Salvation" and consider your final destiny.

The Bible teaches and the history of man is that it takes deliberate effort to do right things and avoid doing wrong things. There is a term in Christian circles "backsliding" which summarizes what happens without constant diligence. But no one has ever heard of someone "front sliding" because it does not happen in this sinful world.

Once the initial decision has been made to follow Christ it takes on-going regular decisions to continue to follow your Savior.

This pyramid is a graphical representation of the steps which I have found useful in my own spiritual walk. Others have also appreciated the pyramid. But while simple in concept it is difficult with regard to on-going application. It takes effort.

The natural course of man works quite smoothly and without effort. First you are presented with a situation where you might think something like, "I shouldn't really do it, but just this once I will." The next time a similar occasion arise you think something like, "I already did that once, and things worked out, so I'll do it a second time." Each time we succumb we are strengthening a new habit – in this case a bad habit. That's how sin works. Little choices eventually become big problems. Little things evolve into big things!

One of the objects of this book is to clarify how everything starts in the mind and then is re-enforced. The question is what are you going to reinforce? Good habits or destructive habits?

May God richly bless and give spiritual insight to each reader.

Closing Scripture

"Blessed be the God and Father of our Lord Jesus Christ, who according to His abundant mercy has begotten us again to a living hope through the resurrection of Jesus Christ from the dead, *to an inheritance incorruptible and undefiled and that does not fade away, reserved in heaven for you*, who are kept by the power of God through faith for salvation ready to be revealed in the last time.

"In this you greatly rejoice, though now for a little while, if need be, you have been grieved by various trials, that the genuineness of your faith, being much more precious than gold that perishes, though it is tested by fire, may be found to praise, honor, and glory at the revelation of Jesus Christ, whom having not seen you love. Though now you do not see Him, yet believing, you rejoice with joy inexpressible and full of glory, receiving the end of your faith — the salvation of your souls.

"Of this salvation the prophets have inquired and searched carefully, who prophesied of the grace that would come to you, searching what, or what manner of time, the Spirit of Christ who was in them was indicating when He testified beforehand the sufferings of Christ and the glories that would follow. To them it was revealed that, not to themselves, but to us they were ministering the things which now have been reported to you through those who have preached the gospel to you by the Holy Spirit sent from heaven — things which angels desire to look into" (1 Peter 1:3-12).

THINK AND GROW

1. Which level of the pyramid provided the most insight to you?
2. If tomorrow you died, how sure are you that your Lord would say to you, "Well done!"
3. Which step of the pyramid do you feel you need to work on the hardest to maintain or hold your gains?
4. Which step on the pyramid are you willing to work hard at

    improving?

        a.   Why did you choose that one?

|||||

Dear Reader,

I would love to hear from you. If you enjoyed this book, you can bless me greatly by posting an honest and candid review wherever you purchased this book (and other sites if you have access). I always read reviews and I would love to hear your thoughts about this book.

In the typical book-buying process, many read reviews of a book prior to purchasing it. It helps them make wise choices in reading. Potential readers are able to make an informed decision about a book by reading what previous readers have to say. Your review would be extremely helpful to future readers and greatly appreciated by me.

Thank you and may God richly bless you.

Robert ("Bob") Lloyd Russell

Appendix A – Text Pyramid Summary

Salvation Decision

The foundation of the pyramid is a deliberate decision to accept Christ's gift of salvation.

~~~~~

DISCIPLESHIP DECISIONS

Salvation results in a call to discipleship (both the "Salvation Decision" and the "Discipleship Decisions" are closely related to "Follow Me").

THINKING

If we are to follow through with our decisions we must consistently think Biblically.

ATTITUDE

Repeated thinking in a particular way creates an attitude.

MOTIVATION

Right attitudes are the most important form of motivation.

ACTION

Our motivations are the key factor driving our actions.

LIFESTYLE

Repeated actions are what determine our lifestyle.

FINISH STRONG
~~~~~

Our progression in a Christ-like lifestyle is what causes us to finish strong.

In the end there will be a time of rewards and potentially hearing our Savior say, "Well done!"

Appendix B – Scripture Pyramid Summary

Salvation

"...whoever believes in Him... has everlasting life." (John 3:16)

~~~~

Discipleship

"...take up his cross, and follow Me." (Mark 8:34)

Thinking

"...be transformed by the renewing of your mind..." (Romans 12:2)

Attitude

Your attitude should be the same as Christ Jesus." (Philippians 2:5)

Motivation

"We love Him because He first loved us" (1 John 4:19)

Action

"Make it your ambition..." (1 Thessalonians 4:11)

Lifestyle

"...Be holy, for I am holy" (1 Peter 1:16)

Finish Strong

"Well done... Enter into the joy of your Lord" (Matthew 25:23)
~~~~

Appendix C – The Simplicity of Salvation

For those who are not sure of their final-destination I would suggest considering what has often been called "The Romans Road" which presents the truth from the Book of Romans in the New Testament.

But first consider that the Bible clearly presents two roads in life. Jesus said, "Strive to enter through the narrow gate, for many, I say to you, will seek to enter and will not be able. When once the Master of the house has risen up and shut the door, and you begin to stand outside and knock at the door, saying, 'Lord, Lord, open for us,' and He will answer and say to you, 'I do not know you, where you are from,' then you will begin to say, 'We ate and drank in Your presence, and You taught in our streets.' But He will say, 'I tell you I do not know you, where you are from. Depart from Me, all you workers of iniquity.' There will be weeping and gnashing of teeth, when you see Abraham and Isaac and Jacob and all the prophets in the kingdom of God, and yourselves thrust out. They will come from the east and the west, from the north and the south, and sit down in the kingdom of God. And indeed there are last who will be first, and there are first who will be last" (Luke 13:24-30).

In a nutshell, one path ends with eternal joy in heaven. The other path, the common popular route, ends in eternal damnation and punishment in hell. The most important decision you can make is to make sure you are on the right road in life. Do it now, because no one, including you, is guaranteed a tomorrow.

The book of Romans was written to people who had a busy lifestyle. They lived in a culture where it was hard to figure out what was true and what was false. How could they make sense of life on this earth? More importantly, what about life after death.

The Romans Road

ONE: Every human everywhere needs a solution to sin. "For there is no difference; for all have sinned and fall short of the glory of God" (Romans 3:22b-23). All have sinned. You do not have to rob hundreds of banks to be found guilty of bank robbery. Rob one bank and you will be found guilty. If you have ever sinned in deed or thought you are guilty before an absolute sinless and righteousJudge.

TWO: Jesus Christ is the only acceptable solution to your sin. "For when we were still without strength, in due time Christ died for the ungodly. For scarcely for a righteous man will one die; yet perhaps for a good man someone would even dare to die. But God demonstrates His own love toward us, in that while we were still sinners, Christ died for us" (Romans 5:6-8).

THREE: Salvation is a gift and it cannot be earned by good works. God doesn't grade on a curve. "For the wages of sin is death, but *the gift of God is eternal life* in Christ Jesus our Lord" (Romans 6:23).

This is a primary difference between salvation through the shed blood of Christ and all religions. *Religions* require that you *do* something to earn your salvation. *Relationship* with Christ is based solely on what He has *done* already for you.

FOUR: True salvation is by God's grace and cannot be earned by your efforts. "And if by grace, then it is no longer of works; otherwise grace is no longer grace. But if it is of works, it is no longer grace; otherwise work is no longer work" (Romans 11:6).

FIVE: Salvation must be accepted by faith. You exercise faith every day in the events of your life—such as driving across a bridge. "But to him who does not work but believes on Him who justifies the ungodly, his faith is accounted for righteousness, just as David also describes the blessedness [happiness] of the man to whom God imputes righteousness apart from works: 'Blessed are those whose lawless deeds are forgiven, and whose sins are covered; blessed is the man to whom the Lord shall not impute sin'" (Romans 4:5-8).

SIX: God will save every person who comes to Him in His prescribed way. "'Whoever believes on Him will not be put to shame.' For there is no distinction between Jew and Greek, for the same Lord over all is rich to all who call upon Him. For 'whoever calls on the name of the Lord shall be saved'" (Romans 10b:11-13).

"It is not your life and your past that determine your life [your eternal destiny]. It is Christ's life and His past that determine your life [eternal destiny]." —Sinclair Ferguson

If you place your trust in Christ "Your robe will be white because Christ's robes were red." —Charles Haddon Spurgeon

Summary

Why not begin your journey along the narrow path, the Romans Road, today? First, recognize that you are a sinner—maybe not as bad as many—but a sinner! How many banks does a person need to rob to be a bank robber? How many sins does a person need to commit to be a sinner?

Second, recognize the truth that God says all sin must and will be judged by God, the Creator.

Third, understand that you are unable to pay the penalty of your sin and satisfy the righteous Judge. No amount of good works will satisfy for payment of sin.

Fourth, understand the Good News that Jesus Christ died in your place and then rose again in payment for the full penalty for your sin.

Finally, accept the free gift of salvation being offered to you—but like any gift it must be accepted.

If you have done so, welcome my brother or sister, into the family of God.

"If you confess with your mouth the Lord Jesus and believe in your heart that God has raised Him from the dead, *you will be saved*. For with the heart one believes unto righteousness, and with the mouth confession is made unto salvation" (Romans 10:9-10).

"And now, if I am a true believer, I stand here freed from every sin. There is not a crime against me in the book of God; it is blotted out forever; it is cancelled; and not only can I never be punished but I have nothing to be punished for. Christ has atoned for all my sins, and I have received His righteousness." ——Charles Haddon Spurgeon

THINK AND GROW

1. If you died tonight are you sure that you would go to heaven?
2. If not, why not reread this Appendix and settle your eternal destiny now?

Additional Thoughts

This book was written with the goal of presenting traditional truths of the Christian faith in a concise and easy-to-understand way. The underlying objective is to bring glory to our great Creator and God.

Many reviewers believe the book accomplishes those goals and should be widely distributed and read. If you agree, please read on.

The publishing world, including the Christian book market, is vastly different than it was even a decade ago. The way books are distributed and sold has been greatly affected. The best way to get the message of this book out to others is through satisfied readers. If you would be willing to help in that endeavor, please consider the following suggestions.

Word of Mouth

Perhaps the most effective means of promoting a book is one satisfied reader telling another.

Internet Buzz

There are many people who are unlikely to be reached except through electronic means. Write an online review of the book.

Write a Review

Post an honest review on the website where you obtained this book (and others). You can also choose to send your review to me at rlr@BOOKSrlr.com

About the Author

Robert Lloyd Russell

Biography

Robert Lloyd Russell's books have won national and international literary awards including a World Book Award (one of just three awards across all genres). He is the editor of a book containing transcribed spoken messages of martyred missionary Jim Elliot. As a small boy Robert lived in the Elliot home at a time prior to Jim's departure for the mission field. The transcriptions were carefully made from old wire recordings, the forerunner of magnetic tape recordings. Jim was one of Robert's Sunday School teachers and Jim's father was one of his spiritual mentors.

Russell has a diverse secular background which spans many functions including engineering, manufacturing, sales, marketing, and staff positions. His technical career included the management of a wide variety of engineers, physicists, and scientists in the high-technology industry.

During the 1970s while he was Camera Engineering Manager for a Fortune 500 corporation, he became fascinated with the attributes of light and the parallels to the attributes of God. He would later write about these parallels in some of his books.

In the early 1970s a senior executive of a major corporation began seeking Robert's opinions and advice. This was the start of a part-time consulting business. Then, from 1990 until his retirement in 2005, Robert devoted his entire career to advising and coaching many executives in a variety of organizations. Based in Portland, Oregon, his consulting practice routinely provided coaching and counseling on a wide range of business issues including ethics, overall effectiveness and profitability, organizational cultural issues, and Total Quality concepts.

During the 1980s as an active Christian businessman concerned about ethics, Robert enrolled in seminary and earned a Master of Christian Leadership degree from Western Seminary. For many years he was a popular adult Sunday School and Bible Study teacher.

Robert refers to himself as a simple **A-B-C** kind of guy: Christian **A**uthor, Christian **B**logger, and Christian **C**onsultant and **C**oach. His blog entitled "Abundant Life Now[1]" has been read in nearly 200 countries and translated into more than 100 languages.

---

1. http://robertlloydrussell.blogspot.com/

Want Free Books?

As an author, I want to thank you for reading *CHRIST'S DISCIPLE: How To Finish Strong"* and I regard the feedback of my readers very highly.

When considering buying a book many people weigh reviews carefully before deciding to purchase. If you enjoyed this book, would you consider assisting me by helping others make an informed decision? Leaving a review (even just a star rating without commentary) can help spread the message of the Gospel and increase others' faith through these books. It is also a great way to support this international ministry.

Robert Lloyd Russell's Newsletter[1]

Sign up for occasional updates from author Robert Lloyd Russell: https://www.subscribepage.com/rlr

He is committed to not bothering you with frequent newsletters. When he does send out occasional communications, it will contain one or more of the following:

- Advance information about current projects
- Related news
- Prayer requests
- Notification of **FREE eBooks** for a limited time
- Other items which may be of interest

(If you decide you no longer want to receive the newsletter, you may take advantage of the "unsubscribe" option at the bottom of each email.)

---

1. *https://www.subscribepage.com/rlr*

|||||

Robert Lloyd Russell's eBooks are available from your favorite online eBook retailer.

You may also want to visit the author's book website Books by Robert Lloyd Russell that lists his eBooks and printed books along with additional information, (booksrlr), or go to Books to Read[2] (https://books2read.com/ap/81Ym5B/Robert-Lloyd-Russell).

|||||

You are invited to connect with Robert Lloyd Russell through his daily internet blog *Abundant Life Now*[3] for inspiration and insight. (http://robertlloydrussell.blogspot.com/)

---

2. https://books2read.com/ap/81Ym5B/Robert-Lloyd-Russell

3. *http://RobertLloydRussell.blogspot.com/*

What To Read Next

"GOD'S NATURE: Sonlight—Sunlight" ISBN: 978-1393359371 ~ ASIN: B083L97PZV ~ Print ISBN: 979-8223228738

An easy-to-read devotional style book which presents new and unforgettable insights. This landmark book identifies fascinating parallels between natural and spiritual light. Analogies teach profound truth in simple language.

"First there was Tozer with *The Knowledge of the Holy,* and then Packer gave us *Knowing God,* and now Russell has taken us further." —Dr. Earl D. Radmacher, General Editor, Nelson Study Bible/New King James Study Bible

Note: This eBook is an update of the first two sections of an earlier print book *GOD LIGHT: Sunlight Sonlight,* which **won six awards**.

Choose your favorite retailer (available in eBook or print)

https://books2read.com/GodsNature

"GOD'S CHILD: Like a Tree" ISBN: 978-1393518266 ~ ASIN: B0874CHLD7 ~ Print ISBN: 979-8215346204

Dr. Ronald B. Allen, a nationally recognized expert on the Psalms, described this book as "The definitive work on Psalm 1."

A timely book for those who long for faster, more consistent spiritual growth. In today's Christian communities many are complacent in their ultimate destination and they neglect the importance of the journey. In so doing, they miss out on many of the here and now benefits of their adoption into the family of God. The normal (not average) Christian is growing more like Jesus Christ as they continue their life on earth. If you long to be a disciple who pleases God, this book is for you. This book is extremely relevant to today's culture.

Choose your favorite retailer (available in eBook or print)

https://books2read.com/GodsChild

"GOD'S CHURCH: *Christ's Pearl*" ISBN: 978-1393268093 ~ ASIN: B07XFPMVQT ~ Print ISBN: 978-1393348597

Early in the book the author provides a straightforward look at the three most popular interpretations of the parable of the pearl of great price. Included is a clear Bible-based rejection of the common notion that the pearl represents salvation.

The major portion of the work provides parallels between the "one pearl of great price" and the Christian Church. Presented are seven unique aspects of a pearl which parallel the uniqueness of the Church. Finally, eight additional characteristics of a pearl and their parallels are presented.

Note: This eBook is an update of an earlier print book *ONE PRECIOUS PEARL: God's Design for His Church,* which **won five awards**.

Choose your favorite retailer (available in eBook or print)

https://books2read.com/GodsChurch

"CHRIST'S DISCIPLE: How To Finish Strong" ISBN: 978-1393844402 ~ ASIN: B091XZF79B ~ Print ISBN: 979-8223262800

Written for those who long for faster, more consistent spiritual growth. Many in today's Christian communities are complacent about their ultimate destination and they neglect the importance of the journey. In so doing, they miss out on many of the here and now benefits of their adoption into the family of God. The normal (not average) Christian is growing more like Jesus Christ as they continue their life on earth. If you long to be a disciple who pleases God, this book is for you.

Choose your favorite retailer (available in eBook or Print).

https://books2read.com/ChristsDisciple

"GOD'S DESIRE: How To Please God" ISBN: 978-1393211785 ~ ASIN: B08H4F619W ~ Print ISBN: 979-8223962915

This book develops two graphic models. The "Christian Life Model" is about victorious Christian living. Included in this section are the author's detailed acrostics for fellowship, obedience, power, prayer, witness, and the Word.

The "Christian Guidance Model" shows the interrelationship of the "Christian Life Model" and one's inner convictions, Godly counsel, and the Lordship of Jesus Christ.

Note: This eBook is an update of an earlier print book *"THY WILL BE DONE ON EARTH: Understanding God's Will for You."*

Choose your favorite retailer (available in eBook or print)

https://books2read.com/GodsDesire

"*GOD'S LIGHT: How To Respond*" ISBN: 978-1393424994 ~ Print ISBN: 979-8223726906

An easy-to-read devotional style book which identifies parallels between the reactions of physical objects to natural light and the reactions of humans to spiritual light. These analogies teach profound truth in simple language.

Written in short easily digestible segments, it is ideal reading for the person on the go. Readers gain a greater appreciation regarding Christians shining like lights.

Note: This eBook is an update of the third section of an earlier print book *GOD LIGHT: Sonlight Sunlight,* which won **six awards**.

Choose your favorite retailer (available in eBook or print)

https://books2read.com/GodsLight

"CHRIST'S BLOOD: 7+ Amazing Benefits" ISBN: 979-8201460877 ~ ASIN: B098W6LHVM ~ Print ISBN: 979-8223389231

Understand the direct benefits to *you* from Christ's death and resurrection.

There are seven (plus one) directly stated benefits in Scripture.

Ponder ten additional benefits resulting from the Cross.

Choose your favorite retailer (available in eBook or print)

https://books2read.com/ChristsBlood

"TEMPTATION" 50+ Tips" ISBN: 979-8201564209 ~ ASIN: B0BCPN5YGW ~ Print ISBN: 979-8223331643

Everyone is tempted (even Christ was)

50+ practical tips for personal victory over temptation!

Understand the battle and your spiritual weapons

Overcome the types of temptations you will face

Be confident and victorious in your Christian life

Choose your favorite retailer (available in eBook or print)

https://books2read.com/temptation-50tips

"PRIDE: Good and Bad" ISBN: 979-8201002053 ~ ASIN: B09SGSQLH9 ~ Print ISBN: 979-8223938781

Achieve a more consistent Christian life

As humans, we all have a common problem. Like rust to steel, pride is to our lives. Although there are examples of good pride in the Bible, most of the time pride is a negative part of our being.

Understanding the problem of pride is a vital part of gaining consistent spiritual victory as we live our daily lives.

Choose your favorite retailer (available in eBook or print)

https://books2read.com/Pride-Good-and-Bad

"SAMSON: Spirit-Controlled to Self-Centered" ISBN: 979-8215866122 ~ ASIN: B0BSZZSY8J ~ Print ISBN: 979-8223612964

The Biblical account of Samson's life includes ten significant victories interspersed among fifteen problematic events. How can we avoid a spiritually fickle life? What are the commonalities and contrasts between the lives of Samson and Christ? How did God evaluate Samson's life?

What practical lessons can we apply to our daily activities by looking at his life?

Choose your favorite retailer (available in eBook or Print).

https://www.booksrlr.com/ebooks/samson/

"PETER: Failure to Faith" ISBN: 979-8223422327 ~ ASIN: B0CBBC7DZC ~ Print ISBN: 979-8223315902

Follow Peter's life in chronological order as he progresses from a fickle follower to a dynamic disciple.

This book can easily be a *fast read*. Due to small segments, it can also be used for *daily devotions* or in *short segments* by busy individuals. For scholars it can be the basis for a *lengthy personal study*. Small groups use it as a *spur to discussions*. Whatever your choice, enjoy as you read and reflect!

Choose your favorite retailer (available in eBook or Print).

https://www.booksrlr.com/ebooks/peter-failure-to-faith/

"*JIM ELLIOT: Recorded Messages*" ISBN: 978-1393887959 ~ ASIN: B088FZ3XSC ~ Print ISBN: 979-8223787563

Note: This eBook is an updated and significantly expanded version of an earlier print book "*JIM ELLIOT: A Christian Martyr Speaks to You.*"

Jim Elliot's spoken words transcribed for you – six practical messages with amazing depth and insight. These messages were given by this martyred Christian missionary before he left for the mission field in Ecuador. They were transcribed from a wire recorder, a forerunner of the magnetic tape recorder.

Christians of all maturity levels benefit from the understanding gained from Jim's discussions.

Choose your favorite retailer (available in eBook or print)

https://books2read.com/JimElliot

Print Book: ISBN: 978-0741475534 ~ ***GOD LIGHT: Sunlight Sonlight*** <u>won six awards</u> and is an easy-to-read devotional style book which presents new and unforgettable insights. This book identifies fascinating parallels between natural and spiritual light, and provides applications of natural and spiritual light. Analogies teach profound truth in simple language.

Available wherever quality print books are sold.

Note: There is an eBook update of the first two sections of this book entitled: "*GOD'S NATURE: Sonlight Sunlight.*" The third section of this book is updated in the eBook entitled: "*GOD'S LIGHT: How To Respond.*" Both are listed previously.

Print Book: ISBN: 978-0741462329 ~ *"ONE PRECIOUS PEARL: God's Design for His Church"* <u>won five awards.</u>

A straightforward look at the three most common interpretations of this parable.

The major portion of the book provides parallels between the "one pearl of great price" and the Christian Church.

Available wherever quality print books are sold.

Note: There is an eBook update of this book is entitled *"GOD'S CHURCH: Christ's Pearl."* It is listed previously.

Print Book: ISBN: 978-1606474310 ~ *"THY WILL BE DONE ON EARTH: Understanding God's Will for You"* is for those who are serious about living life in a way that pleases God.

Through the development of two graphic models the author provides insights regarding the interrelationship of fundamentals of the Christian faith.

Available wherever quality print books are sold.

Note: There is an eBook update of this book entitled *"GOD'S DESIRE: How To Please God."* It is listed previously.

Print Book: ISBN: 978-1615797646 ~ *"JIM ELLIOT: A Christian Martyr Speaks To You"* is directly relevant to all Christians.

Those with an interest in the history of missions or current missions will find the book riveting.

All Christians will appreciate Jim's straightforward, hard-hitting style of speaking.

Available wherever quality print books are sold.

Note: There is an eBook update of this book entitled *"JIM ELLIOT: Recorded Messages."* It has been enhanced and expanded with two additional messages and is listed previously.

Don't miss out!

Visit the website below and you can sign up to receive emails whenever Robert Lloyd Russell publishes a new book. There's no charge and no obligation.

https://books2read.com/r/B-A-QQUI-MRENB

BOOKS 2 READ

Connecting independent readers to independent writers.

Also by Robert Lloyd Russell

Bible Character Series
Samson: Spirit-Controlled to Self-Centered
Peter: Failure to Faith

Christian Concepts Series
God's Church: Christ's Pearl
God's Nature: Sonlight Sunlight
God's Child: Like a Tree

Christian Growth Series
God's Desire: How To Please God
God's Light: How To Respond
Christ's Disciple: How To Finish Strong

Christian Theology Series
Christ's Blood: 7+ Amazing Benefits
Pride: Good and Bad
Temptation: 50+ Tips